BTEC

HEALTH AND SOCIAL CARE

ASSESSMENT GUIDE

Level 2

Unit 1 HUMAN LIFESPAN DEVELOPMENT

Unit 2 HEALTH AND SOCIAL CARE VALUES

CAROLE TROTTER, IAN G...
JOANNE FRANKS, COLLEEN ...
AND MANDY SMAIL...

DISCARDED

D1103512

HODDER
EDUCATION
HACHETTE UK COMPANY

0140230146

The sample learner answers provided in this assessment guide are intended to give guidance on how a learner might approach generating evidence for each assessment criterion. Answers do not necessarily include all of the evidence required to meet each assessment criterion. Assessor comments intend to highlight how sample answers might be improved to help learners meet the requirements of the grading criterion but are provided as a guide only. Sample answers and assessor guidance have not been verified by Edexcel and any information provided in this guide should not replace your own internal verification process.

Any work submitted as evidence for assessment for this unit must be the learner's own. Submitting as evidence, in whole or in part, any material taken from this guide will be regarded as plagiarism. Hodder Education accepts no responsibility for learners plagiarising work from this guide that does or does not meet the assessment criteria.

The sample assignment briefs are provided as a guide to how you might assess the evidence required for all or part of the internal assessment of this unit. They have not been verified or endorsed by Edexcel and should be internally verified through your own Lead Internal Verifier as with any other assignment briefs, and/or checked through the BTEC assignment-checking service.

Orders: please contact Bookpoint Ltd, 130 Milton Park, Abingdon, Oxon OX14 4SB. Telephone: +44 (0)1235 827720. Fax: +44 (0)1235 400454. Lines are open from 9.00a.m. to 5.00p.m., Monday to Saturday, with a 24-hour message answering service. You can also order through our website www.hoddereducation.co.uk

If you have any comments to make about this, or any of our other titles, please send them to educationenquiries@hodder.co.uk

British Library Cataloguing in Publication Data

A catalogue record for this title is available from the British Library

ISBN: 978 1 444 1 8968 1

Published 2013

Impression number   10 9 8 7 6 5 4 3 2 1

Year   2016 2015 2014 2013

Copyright © 2013 Carole Trotter, Ian Gunn, Joanne Franks, Colleen Sawicki and Mandy Smail

All rights reserved. No part of this publication may be reproduced or transmitted in any form or by any means, electronic or mechanical, including photocopy, recording, or any information storage and retrieval system, without permission in writing from the publisher or under licence from the Copyright Licensing Agency Limited. Further details of such licences (for reprographic reproduction) may be obtained from the Copyright Licensing Agency Limited, Saffron House, 6-10 Kirby Street, London EC1N 8TS.

Cover photo © adimas – Fotolia.com

Typeset by Integra Software Services Pvt. Ltd., Pondicherry, India.

Printed in Dubai for Hodder Education,
an Hachette UK Company,
338 Euston Road,
London NW1 3BH

Contents

For attention of the learner

You are not allowed to copy any information from this book and use it as your own evidence. That would count as plagiarism, which is taken very seriously and may result in disqualification. If you are in any doubt at all please speak to your teacher.

Acknowledgments

Photo credits

The authors and publishers would like to thank the following for permission to reproduce material in this book:

p. 3 (bottom) © Imagestate Media (John Foxx); p. 4 (top) © Corbis; (bottom) © Papirazzi – Fotolia; p. 8 (bottom) © Imagestate Media (John Foxx); p. 13 (top) © Jacek Chabraszewski – Fotolia; (bottom) © Jasmin Merdan – Fotolia; p. 19 © laurent hamels – Fotolia; p. 21 © Mark Richardson – Fotolia; p. 22 © Image Source/Getty Images; p. 24 © Monkey Business – Fotolia; p. 26 © auremar – Fotolia; p. 68 © pressmaster – Fotolia. Photos on pp. 2, 3 (top), 5, 10, 15 © Hodder Education.

Every effort has been made to trace and acknowledge ownership of copyright. The publishers will be happy to make suitable arrangements with any copyright holders whom it has not been possible to contact.

Command words

You will find the following command words in the assessment criteria.

Appraise	Consider the positive and negative points and give a reasoned judgement
Assess	Make a judgement on the importance of something – similar to 'evaluate'
Define	Clearly explain what a particular term means and give an example, if appropriate, to show what you mean
Demonstrate	Provide several relevant examples or related evidence which clearly support the arguments you are making. This may include showing practical skills
Describe	Give a clear description that includes all the relevant features – think of it as 'painting a picture with words'
Discuss	Examine a topic in detail, taking into account different ideas and opinions. This could be verbal or written but must be balanced.
Evaluate	Review the information and then bring it together to form a conclusion. Give evidence for each of your views or statements
Explain	Set out in detail the meaning of something, with reasons. More difficult than describe or list, so it can help to give an example to show what you mean. Start by introducing the topic then give the 'how' or 'why'
Outline	Write a clear description but not a detailed one
State	Write a clear and full account

UNIT I
Human Lifespan Development

Unit 1, Human Lifespan Development, is a core unit and the only externally assessed unit for the BTEC Level 2 First Award in Health and Social Care qualification. The learner is assessed through sitting a one-hour, paper-based exam.

The unit provides the opportunity to investigate how humans grow and develop and the impact of the four aspects of human growth and development: physical, intellectual, emotional and social. It also looks at how different events, both expected and unexpected, have an impact on growth and development and the support mechanisms that are available to help manage them.

This unit is divided into two sections. The first section focuses on guidance for the learning aims. All of the topics in the learning aims should be covered in the delivery of the qualification. At the end of each topic there are knowledge recap questions to test your understanding of the subject. The answers for the knowledge recap questions can be found at the back of the guide.

The second section provides guidance on the external exam paper. The exam will last for one hour and is a mixture of different types of questions, including questions requiring a short explanation. Questions are divided into two sections, each section relating to one learning aim. There is a total of 50 marks available – 22 in section A and 28 in section B. The marks awarded for each question or part of a question are clearly shown in bold and in brackets. The guide contains one sample question paper. Sample answers for the question paper are provided at the end of the guide.

Learning aim A
Explore human growth and development across life stages

Learning aim A provides the opportunity to learn about the different stages of growth and development and the key aspects for each life stage.

Topic A.1 The different life stages people pass through during the life course

The life course can be divided into the following stages:

Infancy (birth to 2 years)

Studied ☐

A time when growth is rapid and when a child will learn to crawl, walk, use their hands to move objects and to feed themselves and begin to communicate.

Figure 1.1 Infancy

Early childhood (3–8 years)

Studied ☐

Growth is still rapid but not as rapid as the infancy stage. By the age of eight a child will be able to run, hop, ride a bike, communicate well and join in games.

Adolescence (9–18 years)

Adolescence is a time for physical changes to a child's body and the start of puberty; a time when a child appears grown up but on occasion can be childish. Friends may become more important and influential than family.

Figure 1.2 Adolescence

Early adulthood (19–45 years)

During early adulthood an individual is said to be in peak physical health and fitness. There may be major changes such as gaining employment, marriage and starting a family.

Figure 1.3 Early adulthood

Learning aim A: Explore human growth and development across life stages

Middle adulthood (46–65 years)

Studied ▢

This can be a time for increased responsibilities in caring for children and maybe older family relatives. There may be a decline in physical ability, which is compensated for by knowledge and experience. There will be some physical changes such as men losing their hair or hair turning grey.

Figure 1.4 Middle adulthood

Later adulthood (65+)

Studied ▢

Later adulthood is a time when the body begins to decline and there are problems with mobility and agility. Reactions are slower and although wisdom increases, mental agility can diminish.

Figure 1.5 Later adulthood

It is important to remember that not everyone grows or develops at the same time or in the same way.

UNIT 1 Human Lifespan Development

Topic A.2 Key aspects of human growth and development at each life stage

Physical development

Studied ☐

Physical growth and physiological change will be rapid during the first year and then steady until puberty. It is important to remember that everyone is an individual who may grow and develop at a different time and rate from their peers.

Infancy and early childhood

This is a period of immense growth across all areas of development, from a very dependent newborn baby to a child who, by the age of three, has mastered many skills, including talking, walking, using the toilet, using a spoon and scribbling. **Gross motor skills** will develop – for example, an infant learns how to control their head, sit up and crawl. This life stage also sees the development of **fine motor skills** – for example, an infant learns how to pick up objects or hold a rattle or dummy. A child between the ages of three and five will begin to develop fine-motor skills and by the age of five, most children will be able to use pencils, crayons and scissors. Their gross motor skills should include the ability to skip or hop.

Figure 1.6 A baby showing gross motor skills

Figure 1.7 A baby showing fine motor skills

Adolescence

Between the ages of nine and twelve individual personalities and cognitive skills develop. Growth and development become slower and more steady until the start of puberty. The adolescent years are a period of accelerated growth where individuals become taller and begin to gain weight, although this will vary from individual to individual and across genders. Sexual maturity is one of the most significant developments during this time, although the age at which an individual reaches sexual maturity will vary considerably. Females will often develop faster and reach sexual maturity earlier than males. Both primary and secondary sexual characteristics develop during this life stage. Primary sexual characteristics are those related to reproduction – the sex organs. Secondary sexual characteristics are the features that distinguish males from females, but that are not directly concerned with reproduction. During adolescence females will begin the menstrual cycle, grow pubic hair and their breasts will enlarge; males will see an enlargement of the testes and penis, an increase in body hair and their voices will become deeper.

Early adulthood

This stage is often referred to as the peak years when individuals will have excellent health and coordination and when gross and fine motor skills and sexual activity are at a maximum.

Middle adulthood

During the second stage of adulthood the first signs of the ageing process are the appearance of lines and wrinkles. Women will experience hormone changes, their menstrual cycle will stop and the menopause will begin so they will no longer be able to reproduce. Men may begin to gain weight around the abdomen and women around their hips and thighs. Middle adulthood will see, for both genders, a decline in strength, flexibility and muscle tone and hair loss or thinning or hair turning grey.

Later adulthood

This stage will see the ageing process deepen with more enhanced lines and wrinkles, and blemishes such as age spots and broken vessels will appear. Hair will continue to lose its colour and may become thinner. Some individuals may lose weight or appear smaller as their bones settle and compress. Physical ailments will affect mobility and movement and individuals may experience problems with both their hearing and eyesight. Individuals will experience a decline in both their gross and fine motor skills.

Intellectual/cognitive development across the life stages

Studied ☐

This is how a child will learn and develop thinking and language skills. Intellectual and cognitive development will be influenced by the environment in which a child lives and the experiences they have.

The early years are when a child will develop new cognitive skills including learning language, memory, reasoning and thinking. By the age of two most children have started to speak and will go through several stages before they start using adult language around the age of five or six. A child's moral development is influenced by the people they live and mix with. A child will need to learn how to interact appropriately with others and what acceptable behaviour is. As a child grows and relationships become important, they will begin to think about how they are perceived by others.

By adolescence, a young person will start to think about their future and will have some ability to solve problems in more adult way. Problem-solving skills will continue to develop during adulthood.

In early adulthood, cognitive skills such as memory recall and problem-solving skills are at their peak and people are able to think more abstractly and creatively.

During middle adulthood there is small decline in the ability to perform well in tasks requiring speed and agility but this may be compensated for by increased knowledge and experience.

In later adulthood although verbal skills are retained, memory recall and cognitive skills will continue to decline.

Emotional development across the life stages

Emotional development is learning and developing the emotional skills to live within a family and society. Emotional development is the development of a child's identity and self-image and the development of relationships with family friends and others.

Bonding and attachment

Bonding is the strong attachment that develops between a parent and their baby and what will make the parent want to love and protect their baby. Attachment is the close emotional connection between people and, although it is usually applied to the relationship between a child and their main carer, it is also relevant to relationships between adults. If a child experiences problems with attachments, such as inconsistency in behaviour, long absences or violent behaviour, this may impact on their relationships as they mature and become adults. In adulthood it may be difficult to find a good balance between work and home life and this could have an impact on creating effective bonds and attachments.

Figure 1.8 Bonding and attachment

Security

A small baby provided with consistent care will feel emotionally secure. With regular contact a child can develop strong bonds with others such as grandparents, siblings or friends and when separated from their main carer will still feel safe and secure. Leaving the security of home life can be daunting for a young adult but when the time is right it will provide the opportunity for increased independence and self-reliance. From early adulthood and through to retirement, finding and maintaining employment to provide security for the family will have an impact on emotions.

Figure 1.9 A strong bond with grandparents can help a child feel secure

Self-image

Self-image is how an individual will think and feel about themself and how they imagine other people see them. To adopt a positive self-image means an individual will like who they are and how they look. Having a positive self-image will be about recognising that everyone is unique and different. Adopting a positive self-image will improve self-confidence and interpersonal skills although negative comments from others will impact on self-image. A negative self-image will mean never thinking you are good enough, and this can have an impact on the development of interpersonal skills and confidence and could be responsible for depression or eating disorders.

Self-esteem

Self-esteem concerns the opinions you have and how you feel about yourself. People who have positive self-esteem will find it easier to make friends and will know and accept their strengths and weaknesses. They will feel valued and confident in trying new things. People with negative self-esteem will focus on their weaknesses, the things that have gone wrong and the mistakes they have made. Negative self-esteem could make a person more self-critical so that they find it difficult to deal with problems or are reluctant to try new things. Negative self-esteem could lead to depression, drugs or excessive drinking.

Contentment

Contentment is about feeling satisfied and happy with what you have and what you have achieved. Contentment will mean different things for different people but will happen when self-image and self-esteem are positive.

Social development across the life stages

Social development provides the skills to manage and survive within the family home and the society in which we live.

A child's social development will involve learning how to make friends and become a good friend. In the first few years a child will generally socialise with close family and friends and here is where they will build their confidence and self-esteem and learn how to interact with others. A child will need these skills when they move into nursery, school and later employment and have to interact appropriately with other children and adults.

Figure 1.10 Social development

Between the ages of thirteen and eighteen there will be several important changes in social development with the move from dependent childhood to a more independent adulthood. During adolescence a young person will become more independent of their family and their friendship groups will have a larger impact on the development of their social skills. Adolescence is often seen as a stressful time when conflict may occur with parents and there is the beginning of possible sexual relationships.

Young adults will become socially independent and have a high ambition to succeed. Their social network will change as they begin employment, learn to drive, move away from home, settle down with one partner and plan a family.

Many retired people will have more time and opportunity to join new or different social groups. However, in late adulthood there may be change or decline in social interaction due to mobility problems, finances, or the loss of a long-term partner. A decline in health or mobility may see older adults depending on younger family members and friends for social activities.

Knowledge recap questions

1. State the five life stages.

2. What is meant by the term 'puberty'?

3. Give two examples of fine motor skills.

4. Give two examples of gross motor skills.

5. Describe the likely ageing process in a man aged 58.

6. Explain the differences between abstract and creative thinking.

7. Why do young people learn more quickly than older people?

8. Define self-image.

9. Define self-esteem.

10. Explain why is it important for people to take part in activities that promote independence as well as belonging to friendship groups.

Learning aim B
Investigate factors that affect human growth and development and how they are interrelated

Learning aim B provides the opportunity to learn about the wide range of factors that will have an impact on human growth and development

Topic B.1 Physical factors that affect human growth and development

There are several factors that will have an impact on human growth and development and these will include:

Genetic inheritance

Studied

When a baby is conceived half of their genes will come from their father and the other half from their mother. This means that the baby will have a random mix of their grandparents' genes. This will explain why a child could look like their mother, or more like their grandfather or a sibling. Everybody's genes are unique, unless they are an identical twin, and genes will affect the way an individual looks, their health and the way their body works.

Almost all of a child's physical characteristics, personality traits or a specific talent will come from their genes. Genes will have an impact on academic skills but the environment and the people a child interacts with will also have an impact. Sometimes a parent will have a health disorder or disability that will be passed down to their children. Some health disorders can be inherited and will be passed down from a parent to their children such as cystic fibrosis, autism, Fragile X syndrome and Huntington's disease.

Lifestyle choices

Studied

Lifestyle factors that will have an impact on growth and development include:

- **Diet** – people on a low income may choose food that is cheap to buy but high in sugar and fats. Longer working hours may result in the purchase of fast foods, which are, again, high in sugar and fats. A poor diet could result in obesity and health problems such as heart disease, strokes, diabetes, mobility problems and can reduce lifespan.

- **Exercise** – adults and children who take regular exercise reduce the risk of obesity and this will help prevent heart disease, improve the immune system and help prevent muscle problems.

- **Alcohol** – can be responsible for personality changes, which will affect life both at home and at work. Consumption of alcohol may lead to accidents, violent outbursts and can also be responsible for liver disease or heart problems. If a mother drinks during pregnancy, there is the possibility of a miscarriage, stillbirth, premature birth or a low birth weight.

Figure 1.11 Taking part in exercise will reduce the risk of obesity

- **Smoking** – cigarette smoke contains chemicals that could damage the body cells, and is responsible for causing lung and other forms of cancer. Smoking during pregnancy is said to increase the risk of miscarriage and is linked to lower birth weight and slower development.

- **Drugs** – any drug misuse can have a negative impact on health and is known to be responsible for kidney and liver problems. Illegal drugs may have an impact on behaviour and may cause mood swings, which will impact on life at home and at work.

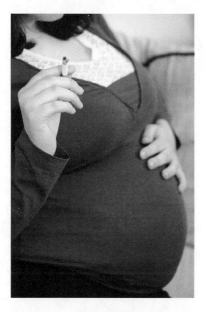

Figure 1.12 Smoking during pregnancy has been linked to lower birth weight and slow development

Illness and disease

A disease is the body's reaction to any disturbance or anomaly in the normal functions of the body. A disease can be anything that will cause an individual pain, distress, social problems or even death.

An illness is more about feeling unwell and is more likely to be temporary, for example, having a cold or a viral infection such as the norovirus. Illness is often the body's reaction to a disease, e.g. diabetes can cause people to feel ill if not controlled properly. Feeling ill or showing signs of illness can be the first signs that a disease is present.

There are several illnesses and diseases that will have an impact on growth and development including:

- Sight or hearing impairments will have an impact on cognitive development and communication skills.
- Down's syndrome, genetic conditions or birth defects could be responsible for slower cognitive development.
- Autism disorders could lead to problems with language and communication.
- Cerebral palsy will impact on muscle development and movement.

Knowledge recap questions

1. Give two examples of genetically inherited factors.

2. Fred is a heavy smoker and wants to improve his lifestyle. Outline the benefits of stopping smoking and taking up exercise.

3. Lauren has picked up a flu virus at school. Is this likely to affect her growth and development? Why?

Topic B.2 Social, cultural and emotional factors that affect human growth and development

There are several social, cultural and emotional factors that can affect human growth and development.

The influence of play

Studied

Play is an essential element in a child's development and it is through play that a child can develop cognitive skills. Play will become the first step in social interaction. Play will develop in stages. Solitary play is the first stage of play, in which the child plays alone. Children progress to social play (which may involve playing alongside another child or an adult), playing with other children, and then on to play that involves planning and rules.

Figure 1.13 Play is important in a child's development

Culture

Studied

From birth and through each stage of human development, culture (religion, spirituality or community influences) will impact on the way we dress, the food we eat and our social interaction. For example, when some Muslim women go out they will wear a dress that covers them from head to foot. Different cultures may exclude a child from participating in some activities. A parent or carer will play an important role in introducing a child to religion and spirituality and will see it as a parenting responsibility to pass on their faith to their children.

Gender

Studied

Young children are aware of the difference between genders. They start to identify themselves in terms of being a boy or girl, which impacts on their dress, the toys they are given and also the way some adults will interact with them. In education, girls are often, for example, guided towards health and social care, which prepares them for motherhood, over engineering or construction. For many years women were seen as mothers and housewives but today young women are choosing a full-time career instead of, before, or as well as having a family. Although women are working longer hours, they are still perceived by many as having the primary responsibility for taking care of the home and family. Despite the introduction of laws to prevent discrimination in the workplace, women may be moving into managerial positions but at the same time often not being paid at the same level as a male colleague.

The influence of role models

Studied

The first role model for any child is their parents and, from a young age, a child will copy and imitate what they see their parents do. The skills and knowledge acquired during childhood and early adulthood will come from learning and observing others. Children and adults will imitate the behaviour of the people they admire. As a child grows, their peers and the social media may influence the way they dress, the food they eat and their views on politics and the environment.

Social isolation

Studied ☐

Social isolation is usually associated with the elderly who are housebound but young mothers and people with disabilities may be affected by the feeling of isolation and loneliness. Social isolation and loneliness could have a negative impact on health, quality of life, self-image and self-esteem.

Knowledge recap questions

1. State two benefits of role models in human development.

2. State two possible problems created by role models in human development.

3. Explain why it is important for children to learn to play with others.

Topic B.3 Economic factors that affect human growth and development

Continual growth and development can be affected by several different economic factors; some will have a positive impact, others a negative one.

Income/wealth

Studied ▢

There is a difference between income and wealth. Income is the money that we get from work, government benefits or investments. It is a flow of money to us. Wealth, on the other hand, is what we inherit or we can create from our income e.g. we can invest our income and earn **more** income from it; or we can inherit wealth such as land from our parents. Wealth can yield an income that is unearned; income used wisely can create wealth. Income is always a money value but wealth may be other assets such as paintings, land or buildings.

People who are born wealthy can often use that wealth to create a better environment for a young person to develop. Income is needed to sustain it.

A child can be raised in a household where there are no money worries and where they are provided with the best designer clothing and the latest electronic gadgets, but high wages and material possessions will be no compensation if there is an absence of the love and time a child needs. A family living on benefits or a low wage may have just enough to pay for the essentials such as rent, heat and food and have nothing left for recreational or social activities. A poor background is often linked to low educational attainment. The impact of low income could be a deprived home environment and poor health. Family life can be affected by the stress and anxiety of trying to keep the family home and to have sufficient money to pay the bills.

Occupation

Studied ▢

Achieving high educational attainments could lead to a professional job role or a managerial position with good pay, pensions, improved housing and increased self-esteem. However, the increased responsibilities in some professional or managerial job roles can result in stress or anxiety. A skilled worker could learn their skills by attending college or university or by receiving on-the-job training. This will provide the opportunity for regular employment, which results in a regular income and money for essentials such as a mortgage or rent, heat and food. A routine job role with similar daily activities can be stress free, but it may lead to a feeling of being trapped, feeling dissatisfied and unhappy and having a low self-image or self-esteem.

Figure 1.14 Being dissatisfied with your job can lead to low self-image

Employment

Studied ☐

Employment will bring financial security but will also help to build confidence and self-esteem. Employment will provide the opportunity to develop work-related and interpersonal skills and to interact with others. It may allow an individual to network and have access to promotional opportunities.

Part-time employment may be the first step to full-time employment but families will often weigh up the benefits of having a higher income against the disruption to family life of full-time work. Employment will have a positive impact on the money coming into the home but long working hours and travel could have a negative impact on quality time spent with partners and children.

Securing full-time employment is one way to resolve money issues but there may be a lack of available employment opportunities in the local area. To access employment, an applicant will need basic and work-related skills and is often required to have relevant industry-related experience. The longer someone is out of work, the lower their chance of getting back into work. Lack of confidence and self-esteem or health problems can prevent people from seeking employment but the consequences of being unemployed can also contribute to physical and mental ill-health. High unemployment and struggling with financial problems can result in an increase in crime and the breakdown of relationships.

Knowledge recap questions

1. What is the difference between part-time employment and seasonal employment?
2. What is the difference between a job and an occupation?

Topic B.4 Physical environment factors that affect human growth and development

There are several factors that affect human growth and development and these include the environment in which they live.

Housing conditions

Studied ▢

Adults on low income or with no secure income may have to live in poor neighbourhoods. A deprived area or poorly maintained housing conditions can have a negative impact on the mental and physical health of the family. A family may live in housing that is substandard, damp, cold and overcrowded and therefore be more susceptible to health problems. Noisy, poor and overcrowded conditions could affect learning and this will impact on academic achievements and employment opportunities. Infections and illness from poor housing conditions will result in absence from school and this will impact on learning and will increase the possibility of unemployment or low-paid employment opportunities. A child's values and behaviour will be learnt from life at home, and in poor areas where there is high unemployment and increased levels of petty crime a child could have behavioural problems and lower educational attainment.

Figure 1.15 Coming from a deprived background could affect development

Pollution

Studied ▢

An increase in the population brings an increase in the amount of waste and pollution, which will have a negative impact on human health. Industrial smoke and exhaust fumes from vehicle engines contain different chemicals or emissions and when breathed in can be the cause of many health problems, including problems with the respiratory system. Industry, agriculture and landfills have been identified as sources of water pollution. People can get typhoid or cholera from drinking contaminated water. Stress caused by noise pollution from traffic, aircraft and rowdy people is linked to heart attacks and strokes.

Figure 1.16 Living near industry can cause health issues

Knowledge recap questions

1. What is the difference between income and wealth?

2. What is meant by 'security of income'?

3. Explain how poor living conditions such as poor sanitation can impact on health.

Topic B.5 Psychological factors that affect human growth and development

Several psychological factors can affect human growth and development.

Relationships with family members

Studied ☐

A family is a group who are related to one another. The family structure could be:

- parents and their children
- single parent and their children
- extended families with parents, children and grandparents
- reconstituted families where a couple are not both the parents of each child in the family.

Family can be one of the most important elements of life and one that provides security, the feeling of belonging and a place where family members find comfort and support. All family members should be made to feel special and many will rely, in many life stages, on family members for social and emotional support. To help build confidence and self-esteem, parents need to provide unconditional love and support for their children. Family members can be responsible for teaching and guiding younger children and for providing the support and guidance that allow family members to achieve their individual goals and ambitions. Family members should feel comfortable in expressing opinions and deal effectively with rows and arguments. Some families are very close; others, when family members get older, will relocate and may grow apart from some or all members of the family.

Figure 1.17 Family is an important element of life

Unconditional acceptance of someone within the family grouping is to embrace them without any strings attached. There is no agenda of "I will accept you if you do....". It is most often seen in parents for children. This acceptance is based on **understanding** the person involved, **appreciating** their outlook and personality and **embracing** what they do as being a part of what they are.

Sometimes the phrase "warts and all" is used to describe this unconditional acceptance. During difficult times parents might disagree with what a child does but they still love them for what they are and will still love them just the same.

Animals often show unconditional love and acceptance towards their owners. It's just love with nothing wanted or needed in return.

Growing up in care

`Studied`

When it is not possible for a child to be brought up by their parents because of illness, an unstable family environment or a death, they could be taken into care and either adopted or fostered. Adoption is providing a new family for a child who cannot be brought up by their parents. Foster care is a temporary home, for a few days or years, until the child can be returned to their parents or is placed for adoption. A child in foster care may have regular contact with their parents. A child brought up in care may feel abandoned and this will impact on their self-image and self-esteem. A child who is fostered or adopted may feel rejected and this could result in them being too eager to please or being angry and defiant. Some children will find social interaction difficult and will be reluctant to accept help, which could impact on educational achievements.

Friendship patterns and relationships with partners

`Studied`

Friendships can develop from a young age and are usually between people with similar interests, values and beliefs. Friends are the people who will listen to you, encourage you and support your decisions but who will not be afraid to say when ideas and plans are wrong. Friends will be people who can be depended on and who provide emotional support during the good and the bad times. Friends will accept a person for who they are and because they are prepared to listen to problems, they can help reduce stress levels and blood pressure.

In relationships with partners, the friendship element is important. Partners should provide unconditional love and trust and be there to listen, encourage and support. Positive relationships can promote positive self-image and high self-esteem.

Stress

Stress can have both a negative or positive impact on life. Stress, in small quantities, can have a positive impact and can help people perform well, stay focused and motivate them to do better. Everyone will deal with stress differently but at a certain stage stress ceases to be beneficial and begins to affect health. Stress can be caused by a wide range of events such as unemployment, divorce or relationship problems, family or work-related problems. Stress can be responsible for health issues, changes in mood and behaviour, a decline in productivity and problems with relationships at home and at work. Stress can be responsible for problems with concentration and memory problems and for eating and sleeping disorders.

Figure 1.18 Stress can be responsible for health issues

Knowledge recap questions

1. Define the term 'unconditional acceptance'.

2. Jim's parents died when he was a baby. He grew up in care. How might this have affected his relationships with other people?

Topic B.6 The expected life events that can affect human growth and development and the positive and negative effects of the events on growth and development

In life there are many events and challenges that should be enjoyable but which often can be stressful.

Starting, being in and leaving education

Studied ▢

Starting school can be a big challenge and not one that every child will enjoy. Children who have constantly been with their parent may feel daunted by the separation of being at school. A child, and their parents, will feel anxious about starting school but parents can help children by talking positively about school and making sure a child is well prepared by knowing how to dress themselves and use the toilet. Starting school will be a time for meeting new people, experiencing different dress codes and encountering new rules.

At the age of eleven a child will often move from a small primary school to a much larger secondary school or academy. Many will be nervous and worried about moving from a familiar environment to a new school with more people, different subjects and new rules.

A child will spend at least twelve years in school. Some will enjoy school and want to continue in education and others cannot wait to leave. When the time comes to leave school the uncertainty about what to do can be confusing for some and exciting for others.

Moving house/location

Studied

Moving house or location is a big upheaval for all the family and for adults is said to be one of the most stressful times of their lives. A child will feel anxious about moving away from a familiar environment, leaving their home and their friends. A child will need to be prepared for the move and some may feel excited, whilst others may demonstrate signs of anxiety or anger. For children of school age, who may not understand the need to move, there could be the stress of starting at a different school and making new friends. For a teenager the move may mean being separated not only from their important circle of friends but also being separated from a boyfriend or girlfriend. The stressful separation from friends and the move of schools may result in the teenager displaying anger, aggression and disruptive behaviour.

Figure 1.19 Moving house can be a big upheaval for a family

Entering and being in employment

Studied

Starting a new job can be similar to the first day at school – exciting but stressful. The unfamiliar environment will make the new employee feel nervous and uncomfortable. The new employee will need to learn and understand workplace rules and develop and build positive working relationships with colleagues. A new job will bring new daily routines and this may mean a longer working day, different meal times and travel arrangements.

Living with a partner/marriage/civil ceremony

Studied

Many people will choose to marry their partners but others show their commitment by moving in together. Planning a wedding or civil ceremony can be stressful and is a time for feeling nervous and tense but excited. Preparing for the day may cause eating and sleeping disorders and could have an impact on concentration at work. Marriage or living with a partner is said to provide emotional support, which will reduce depression and stress.

Parenthood

Studied

Most parents will be delighted and happy when their baby is born but parenthood will bring changes to their daily routines and their relationship. Parents will find it stressful coping with the demands of a new baby and the change to their normal daily routine. A dad may begin to feel isolated, unimportant and ignored because the mother is dealing with the needs and demands of the new baby. The new mother may be tired, stressed, anxious and irritable due to disturbed sleep patterns and coping with her new role.

Retirement

Studied

The right time for leaving employment and retirement will vary but many will see it as the time for relaxing and for fulfilling dreams. Retirement will remove the worry of work-related problems but could still be stressful due to ill-health and loneliness. Leaving work may remove the opportunity for social interaction, leaving an individual feeling isolated, depressed and redundant. Stress-related problems are said to be reduced if the retired person is married. Implementing a daily routine that includes different activities and social interaction will help improve emotional and health issues.

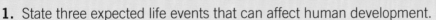

Knowledge recap questions

1. State three expected life events that can affect human development.

2. Describe two positive effects of moving to a new house.

3. Describe two negative effects of retirement.

Topic B.7 The unexpected life events that can affect human growth and development and the effects of the events on personal growth and development and that of others

Death of a partner, relative or friend

Studied ☐

Everyone will react differently to the death of a family member or a friend. They will have a feeling of sadness and loneliness, but could also feel angry or guilty. People who have lost close family or friends could have problems with eating, sleeping and concentration. Some may want to talk about the deceased whilst others may want to avoid discussing them. Some may find it easier to communicate their feeling than others and although death will affect someone emotionally, they may be reluctant to show their feelings.

Accidents, injury and ill-health

Studied ☐

An accident, injury or ill-health can often be sudden and will impact on both the individual and their family. Family life will be disrupted and family members will be upset, feel helpless and anxious. An accident or an illness may mean temporary or permanent changes to roles and responsibilities in the home and any future plans and dreams. Recovering from an accident or illness will be stressful and this may cause aggression, anger or changes in behaviour that will impact on all family members.

Exclusion or dropping out of education

Studied ☐

Exclusion from education is when a child is told they cannot attend school either for a set period of time or permanently. A child is usually only permanently excluded when there are persistent behaviour issues or for a serious offence. A child who is excluded or who drops out of education could be limiting their prospects of finding employment. Having no basic skills or qualifications could result in unemployment or low-paid employment, which could lead to living in a neighbourhood with poor housing conditions. Living in a poor or deprived neighbourhood could lead to experimenting with drugs and drink and petty crime.

Imprisonment

Studied

When a parent is sent to prison there is a major impact on other members of the family, especially their partner and children. Family members will experience fear, anger, embarrassment and anxiety about the future. The family may suffer financially, lose their home and occasionally a child may be taken into care. A child will be anxious and angry and this could result in behaviour problems at home and school. The separation of being in prison, especially a long sentence, could impact on relationships.

Promotion, redundancy and unemployment

Studied

Promotion at work is what motivates most people to perform well but an increase in workload and responsibilities can be the cause of increased stress and anxiety.

Redundancy is out of the control of most employees but many will feel embarrassed and responsible for the impact it will have on their families. A person can feel grief, depression and anger after redundancy and this could affect their relationships with family members and friends. Redundancy and unemployment will be stressful and cause anxiety and worries, both financially and for the future.

Unemployment happens when you no longer have a job and so there is a reduction in earnings. Unemployment is usually involuntary and can be caused by being sacked or made redundant. It is often unexpected and so can cause a lot of stress on families.

Knowledge recap questions

1. State three unexpected life events that can affect human development.

2. Describe two positive effects of being made redundant.

3. Describe two negative effects of dropping out of education.

Topic B.8 Understanding how to manage the changes caused by life events

Types of support

Studied

There are different types of support available and these include:

- **Informal support** – from parents, grandparents, family members, other parents and friends.
- **Formal support** – from doctors, social workers, district nurses, local organisations such as parent support groups.
- **Emotional support** – this can be provided by family and friends but at times there may be the need to seek professional support when dealing with problems such as mental illness, depression or stress.
- **Physical support** – providing support with physical activities and mobility.

Support offered by people

Parents, family members and friends will play an important role in providing emotional support and guidance for both children and adults. When more professional advice and support are required, there are several national and local organisations who are on hand to help. Support and guidance are available in many areas including childcare, care for the elderly, parenting groups, unemployment, adoption and fostering and counselling for bereavement.

Professional support and advice may be required for people who have stress-related or emotional problems following accidents, bereavement, redundancy or the breakdown of a marriage. Physical support may be required for someone who has mobility problems or who cannot manage routine day-to-day activities.

To remain living at home, rather than hospital, certain people will need to access and depend on professional care services. A district nurse and social care workers will provide care and training to help people, whenever possible, maintain their independence and improve their quality of life. A district nurse will monitor the

Figure 1.20 Offering support

UNIT 1 Human Lifespan Development

health needs and home environment of the elderly, people with disabilities or terminal illness and patients released from hospital. A social care worker will provide support and guidance for the elderly, adults with mental or physical disabilities, adults and children in unstable homes, young offenders and vulnerable children.

Support offered by community groups, voluntary and faith-based organisations

Groups can be set up in the local community to provide a meeting place and emotional support for families. Community groups will provide meeting places and support for parents, the elderly and people with disabilities. Voluntary groups rely on charitable donations to provide help and support in the local community. Faith-based organisations, made up of people who have the same beliefs and values, are predominantly set up to provide food, clothing and shelter to people in need.

Managing expectations

Studied

Striving to achieve expectations can be stressful and failing to achieve expectations can result in anger and frustration. Having unrealistic expectations of others can also result in disappointment. To maintain a healthy life it is important to have realistic expectations of yourself and others, accept that everyone can have a bad day, understand that mistakes can be made and lessons can be learnt. Having expectations that cannot be achieved will lead to disappointment and low self-esteem but success, no matter how small, will improve self-image and self-esteem. Managing expectations can come from having smaller, achievable ambitions and being able to openly discuss expectations with partners and friends.

Knowledge recap questions

1. How does a community group differ from a faith-based organisation?

2. Explain why it is sometimes easier to talk with a social care worker than with a member of the family?

Unit 1 External assessment: sample paper

Information
- The total mark for this paper is 50.
- The marks available for each question are shown in brackets.

UNIT 1 Human Lifespan Development

Section A

1. The following information is about the Frost family. Read the information and answer the questions below.

   Cherry is a 65-year-old grandmother. She is married to Geoff.

   They have a daughter, Ariadne, who is 40. Ariadne has two daughters: Katherine, 8, and Isabella, 12.

   Ariadne works full-time as the manager of a high-class jewellers.

   The girls attend a private school.

   (a) State Cherry's current life stage. (1)

   (b) State Katherine's current life stage. (1)

2. Cherry enjoys knitting and, with other enthusiasts, has founded the Sareen Knitting Circle.

(a) Give **one** reason why this is important for Cherry's physical development. **(1)**

(b) Other than physical development, give **two** examples of how knitting could help Cherry in her current life stage. **(2)**

3. Isabella is 12. She is entering puberty.

(a) Define the term 'primary sexual characteristics'. **(1)**

(b) Give **two** examples of these. **(2)**

(c) Give **two** examples of secondary sexual characteristics. **(2)**

(d) Outline **two** ways Isabella will show increasing sexual maturity. **(2)**

4. Ariadne has been made redundant from her job.

She has been offered a part-time job at a school but this is not enough to pay the household bills.

She has taken an extra job as a cleaner at the home of one of Katherine's friends.

(a) Give **two** possible effects on Ariadne's emotional development as a result on this change of job. **(2)**

(b) Give **two** positive effects on Ariadne's intellectual development. **(2)**

(c) Explain how Ariadne's new employment status might affect her daughters. **(6)**

(TOTAL for Section A = 22 marks)

Section B

1. Ian is married to Mary who is 11 years older than him. They had a son soon after they married.

   When he was at university Ian developed anorexia. After 10 years of marriage Ian took up long-distance running. He lost a lot of weight as result of this.

   (a) Explain how this lifestyle change affected Ian. **(2)**

   (b) Anorexia is an illness. Outline the difference between an illness and a disease. **(2)**

2. Ian became obsessed with training and running. Sometimes he would be training when Mary thought he was at work.

(a) Give **two** negative impacts this might have on his family. **(2)**

(b) Explain how these impacts might affect Ian's family. **(4)**

3. Mary is a teacher. She is 51 and enjoys an active lifestyle, particularly adventure sports such as mountaineering. She been told she needs a pacemaker after a defect was found in her heart when she had been taken ill.

(a) Describe **two** physical factors that may affect Mary in the future. **(2)**

(b) Describe **two** psychological factors that Mary may have to cope with. **(2)**

(c) Appraise the support Mary can access in managing the changes to her lifestyle. **(8)**

4. Mary and Ian have both decided to retire. They are both healthy and enjoy history. Their son lives in New Zealand.

(a) Evaluate the likely changes to Mary and Ian's lifestyle following their retirement. (6)

(TOTAL for Section B = 28 marks)

UNIT 2
Health and Social Care Values

Unit 2, Health and Social Care Values, is an internally assessed core unit with two learning aims. It provides the opportunity to investigate how care values are applied in health and care services. The unit provides an introduction to the importance of a duty of care and how the health and social care services are regulated. Learning aim B focuses on the methods used to empower individuals who use the health and care services. The unit introduces why the person-centred approach encourages independence and improves self-confidence and self-esteem.

This unit is divided into three sections:

- The first section focuses on guidance for the two learning aims. All of the topics in the learning aims should be covered in the delivery of the qualification.
- The second section provides support with assessment by using evidence generated by a learner, for each grading criterion, with feedback from an assessor. The assessor has highlighted where the evidence is sufficient to satisfy the grading criterion and provided developmental feedback when additional work is required.
- The third section includes sample assignment briefs for this unit. The unit has been covered by two assignment briefs: the first focuses on learning aim A; the second assignment brief covers learning aim B. The assignment briefs provide the learner with clear guidance on the evidence they will need to generate and submit for the grading criteria, and clearly identifies the format in which the evidence should be submitted.

Answers to the knowledge recap questions in this unit can be found at the back of the guide.

Learning aim A

Explore the care values that underpin current practice in health and social care

Anyone working in health and social care should have an awareness of the values that are important when working with the (often vulnerable) individuals who are using care facilities. It is important to understand the impact of effective and ineffective application of these values in health and social care. You will have the opportunity to demonstrate the practical application of the care values in selected health and social care contexts.

Assessment criteria

2A.P1	Describe how care values support users of services, using relevant examples.
2A.P2	Demonstrate the use of care values in selected health and social care contexts.
2A.M1	Discuss the importance of the values that underpin current practice in health and social care, with reference to selected examples.
2A.D1	Assess the potential impact on the individual of effective and ineffective application of the care values in health and social care practice, with reference to selected examples.

Topic A.1 Defining and demonstrating care values

Confidentiality

People who work in health and social care will have access to personal information about the people they care for and it is their responsibility to ensure that this information is only shared when necessary. To implement appropriate care and support, there will be times when people who work in health and social care services will have to share patients' personal details with colleagues and other professionals. However, personal information on individuals who use health and social services should never be passed on without the individual's consent and permission.

There needs to be a relationship of trust between the people working in health and social care services and the individuals who use their services. Confidentiality is important and should ensure that information on individuals is only accessible to those authorised to have access to it.

When a child, young person or vulnerable adult is at risk and it is difficult to obtain consent, or consent is refused, information will be shared to prevent harm or remove risks.

To provide effective health and social care support, it is important that accurate records are maintained and regularly updated. To maintain confidentiality, records that are stored electronically should be password protected with restricted access. Paper files should be stored in locked filing cabinets that can only be accessed by authorised staff.

Figure 2.1 Paper files should be stored in filing cabinets

There are laws which protect confidentiality including:

- **Data Protection Act 1998** – this law states that information should be kept secure and only used for the purpose for which it was obtained.
- **Human Rights Act 1998** – this law states that everyone has the right to have their private life respected, and this includes the right to keep your health records confidential.

Dignity

Dignity is often linked with receiving respect from others, having privacy and independence. People involved in providing health or social care have a duty to respect and preserve the dignity of their patients and encourage self-respect.

Communication and getting to know the individual, and not dismissing their views and opinions, are important factors which will contribute to maintaining self-respect and dignity.

An individual will often be using the health and care services when they are vulnerable and may often need support with personal tasks such as bathing, using the toilet, eating or drinking. Care and support should be provided but the individual should never be made to feel embarrassed. An adult will feel that their dignity is being undermined if they are treated like a child.

Figure 2.2 Individuals should be treated with dignity

Respect for the individual

Everyone using the health and social care services should be treated as an individual and should never be labelled by their age, illness or disability. Health and social care providers should understand the feelings and the wishes of the people they are caring for and never make assumptions. They should adopt a non-discriminatory and non-judgemental approach to practice. The attitude and behaviour of care services should encourage individuality and any service provided should be personalised to meet the need of the individual.

Other factors which will help individuals maintain their dignity and respect are:

- Involving the individual in making decisions about their lives, care and the support they will need.
- Developing effective communications – providing clear information but listening to the views of the individual without making assumptions.
- Using language that an individual will understand, and never using jargon.
- Not making assumptions about gender, culture, age or disability.
- Asking how the individual would prefer to be addressed and respecting their wishes.
- Awareness and respect of issues of sensitivity that relate to modesty, gender, culture or religion.
- Ensuring that the modesty of patients and clients is protected but also respecting cultural differences.
- Knocking before entering rooms.
- Knowing and understanding the needs of different cultures.
- Providing support to maintain personal hygiene and appearance but respecting personal preference to products and routine.
- Respecting the choice of dress.
- Ensuring that food and drink is sufficient for the individual but taking into consideration individual dietary needs and food preferences. When necessary providing discreet support.
- Ensuring that individuals have access to medication.
- Providing privacy for individuals to use the toilet and the bathroom.
- Encouraging and providing support with social interaction.
- Providing support to maintain their living environment.
- Resolving any problems quickly.

Safeguarding and duty of care

People who are employed in the health and social care services will be responsible for keeping the people they work with safe. This includes ensuring both the physical and emotional safety of individuals, including ensuring that negligence is avoided.

Physical safety involves anyone in a responsible position to develop plans, create systems such as risk assessment to minimise the risk of danger. The next step is to train staff on how to prevent, deter, detect, and respond to these situations. Prevention is always better than solution but if a solution is needed then the response needs to be quick, appropriate and successful. Lessons learned from situations need to be used to improve on what already exists wherever possible.

Emotional safety usually refers to relationships with other people. If people feel emotionally safe, they trust each other, or others, and routinely give each other the benefit of the doubt in questionable situations. Similarly they are willing to share worries and act upon advice given by those they trust. When emotional safety is lost people become wary and distrustful; they feel let down and become unwilling to take the 'risk' of trusting anyone again.

People in positions of responsibility need to ensure those for whom they are responsible feel emotionally safe e.g. by maintaining confidentiality where appropriate; by giving sound advice that is person-centred; by not allowing prejudice to become part of any discussions.

Duty of care is a legal obligation to work by set standards, as far as it is reasonable to do so, in order to prevent any harm or danger to individuals in their care. Service providers are responsible for the safeguarding of the vulnerable people they work with. Maintaining standards and a safe environment could prevent harm or risks to individuals who depend and rely on the service provided by professionals working in health and social care services.

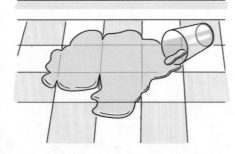

Figure 2.3 It is important to maintain a safe environment

Codes of Practice

The regulator of social workers and social work education in England was previously the General Social Care Council (GSCC), which closed on 31 July 2012. The register of social workers transferred to the Health and Care Professions Council (HCPC) (previously the Health Professions Council (HPC)). The HCPC was set up to protect the health and well-being of the people who use health and social services and maintains a register of all health and care professionals who satisfy their standards. The HCPC is an independent regulator for professions such as paramedics, social workers in England, physiotherapists and speech and language therapists. If a registrant does not meet the required standards, action can be taken, which may include stopping them from practising.

The **Health and Social Care Act 2008 (Regulated Activities) Regulations 2010** are the regulations that ensure that health and adult social care in England satisfies essential quality and safety standards. Health and social care providers are continually monitored to ensure that individuals receive a quality and safe service and maintain self-respect and dignity.

The role of the **Care Quality Commission** is to check that the care and treatment provided by hospitals, dentists, care homes and care services provided for individuals at home are meeting and maintaining national standards. The Commission will monitor the treatment and care provided by hospitals, dentists, the ambulance service and the services for mental health care. They will also monitor the service and care provided for care homes and for individuals who live at home. The monitoring of National Standards is by regular visits to the health and social care providers. National Standards cover all care elements, including treating individuals with dignity and respect and maintaining a clean and safe environment.

Legislation

The **Mental Capacity Act (2005)** was set up to ensure that individuals were empowered to make as many life-changing or routine decisions for themselves as possible. The Act outlines that everyone is assumed to have the capacity to make decisions unless proved otherwise and that when decisions are made for an individual who lacks capacity, they are done in the best interest of the individual.

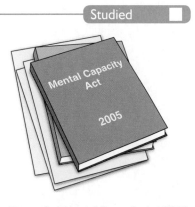

The **Human Rights Act 1998** was introduced to ensure that everyone is treated equally, fairly, and with dignity and respect. Everyone should be protected from harm or danger and cared for in ways that they choose.

Figure 2.4 Mental Capacity Act 2005

Professional practice

Studied ☐

People who work in the health and social care services have an important role to play in safeguarding individuals. They will work in partnership with other professionals to secure sufficient resources to meet the needs of individuals who use care services and maintain standards of good practice.

Excellent communication channels should be established and provide sufficient and up-to-date advice to all relevant people and organisations. Effective communication is essential in building and maintaining relationships with the individual, colleagues and other professionals. Correct procedures should be implemented that comply with legislation on the storage and forwarding of individuals' personal information.

Working in a health and social care role will require adopting an approach that meets the needs of the individual and an understanding of their beliefs and values.

People employed in health and social care service should regularly reflect on the service they provide and be able to adapt to changes in the needs of the individual and the environment. It is important that anyone working in the sector is up to date with organisational practices in their place of work and any changes in relevant legislation or national standards.

A person-centred approach to care delivery

Studied ☐

A **person-centred approach** is making the individual the main focus and involves:

- planning with the individual rather than planning for them
- ensuring decisions are made with the individual and not for them
- providing the support that will allow the individual to live how they want.

Figure 2.5 Involving an individual in their care

A person-centred approach focuses on treating people as individuals, allowing them to make decisions and choices about their care. It will involve listening to what an individual wants and understanding what is important to them. A person-centred approach will make the individual feel more in control of their own life and have a choice in how they are supported.

Knowledge recap questions

1. What is meant by the term 'confidentiality'?

2. State three rules of confidentiality.

3. Lily has told the school nurse she is pregnant. Why must this information remain confidential?

4. What is meant by a non-discriminatory approach?

5. What is meant by a non-judgemental approach?

6. Why might you use the term 'Ms' when speaking with a woman you have just met?

7. Colin is a social worker with responsibility for several elderly people. Why should he **not** tell the people he visits about his own illnesses?

8. Explain the term 'duty of care'.

9. Explain what is meant by the term 'safeguarding' in a health and social care situation.

10. What is the difference between physical and emotional safety?

Assessment guidance for Learning aim A

2A.P1 **Describe how care values support users of services, using relevant examples.**

Assessor report: The command word for 2A.P1 is **describe**. This means give a clear description that includes all the relevant features of how care values support users of services.

The question asks you to describe values in plural. This means that, to achieve 2A.P1, the learner will need to describe how all of the care values listed in the unit content support users of services.

✍ Learner answer

There are a range of values within health and social care that support users of services.

Confidentiality is one of these values. It will keep users safe by making sure that personal information does not get into the wrong hands.

Dignity is another value which can support users of services. This makes sure that users are treated with respect.

Another example of values that support users of services is safeguarding. One way that this can be carried out is by following professional practice, such as listening to what users are communicating.

Assessor report: The learner has listed three examples of values that are used in health and social care (confidentiality, dignity and safeguarding). However, these are not fully described. The learner should now provide more detail on what each value actually is, and how each value supports users of services. They should include at least one relevant example for each value.

Learner answer

Confidentiality ensures that users' personal information is handled correctly and in line with the rules of confidentiality. These rules state that users' records should be stored securely – for example, in a locked filing cabinet in an office or on a password-protected computer. **(a)** Users' personal information should not be discussed with inappropriate people and written permission should be sought by the user before any personal information is passed on to other services.

Another value is dignity. This value ensures appropriate action is taken to preserve the dignity of individuals, by respecting the individual and having a non-judgemental approach. An example of this is not judging people based on their background. **(a)** Dignity also includes finding out how to address an individual, making sure the individual is addressed in the way that they wish to be. For example, in a care home the elderly may wish to be called 'Mr Black' rather than 'James'. **(a)** Dignity also ensures that a user's cultural and religious requirements are met. For example, this could be providing kosher food for a person of the Jewish religion. **(a)**

Safeguarding is also a value which supports service users. This involves ensuring that the physical and emotional safety of individuals is met. An example of this is ensuring that services users are treated in a professional way, ensuring a relationship built upon trust and respect is established and that people feel emotionally secure in their environment. This can include making sure a building is secure so that users do not feel threatened by outsiders. **(a)**

Assessor report: The learner has described how three care values support users of services. They have included relevant examples for each value **(a)**. They have not described how a person-centred approach to care delivery supports users of services.

What is good about this assessment evidence?

The learner has provided good descriptions of how confidentiality, dignity and safeguarding support users of services. They have provided at least one relevant example for each value.

What could be improved in this assessment evidence?

To achieve 2A.P1, the learner needs to describe how all of the values listed in the unit content support users of services. In their answer they have not described how a person-centred approach to care delivery supports users of services. To achieve 2A.P1, they will need to provide a similar level of detail for this as they have for the other care values, providing at least one relevant example.

2A.P2 Demonstrate the use of care values in selected health and social care contexts.

Assessor report: The command verb for this grading criterion is **demonstrate**. To achieve this, learners will need to provide several relevant examples or related evidence that clearly supports the use of care values in health and social care contexts. Learners could provide evidence for this demonstration through a reflective log, which has been completed whilst on practical placements. Learners should demonstrate understanding of how the values are used in at least two settings with different service users or groups. If placement is not practical, then role play can be an alternative way of assessing this, with the use of recording equipment and peer and assessor feedback.

 Learner answer

Reflective log

Whilst I have been studying health and social care I have been on two placements. One was in a care home for the elderly and the other one was a day care facility for children. On Monday 8 November I attended a placement in a local care home for the elderly, this placement lasted for a week. In the last week, beginning 25 April, I attended a local children's day nursery for one week. During my time there I completed diary entries every time I witnessed the care values in place. **(a)**

Upon arrival at both placements I was asked to show my CRB (police check) and photographic identification before I was admitted into the main buildings – this is security, which is part of safeguarding the service users.

I asked how confidentiality was put into place and was told that the service users' personal notes were kept in the office.

As I settled into the daily routine of the care home, I learnt that each resident had been assigned key workers to meet their personal needs on each shift. This ensured that every individual's needs were being fully met. Some service users preferred to make choices for themselves, such as what they were going to wear that day. This demonstrates the care value of a person-centred approach and respect for the individual.

Assessor report: The learner has provided a good introduction, which identifies the two different health and social care settings that they will refer to when demonstrating their use of care values **(a)**.

The learner has demonstrated some good observations of care values in a care home. However, some development of points would strengthen the demonstration of care values experienced. The reflections are limited and rely more on what the learner was told and observed. It would be advantageous for the learner to write about their own personal experiences that involve the use of the care values. For instance, was the student shown any care plans or developmental records? Did they take part in activities with the service users? Which care values did they see put into place during these activities?

The learner has not so far considered all of the care values – they have only referred to safeguarding, confidentiality, respect for the individual and a person-centred approach to care.

Although they refer to two different settings, the demonstration so far is limited to one context. To achieve 2A.P2, they will need to demonstrate the use of care values in both settings.

As well as service users' care plans and personal notes being kept in the office, only people who needed to know this information viewed them. The notes were kept in a filing cabinet and this was usually locked. I was only given information about the residents that would be beneficial to me helping the service users. This showed that confidentiality was in place.

During an activity in the day room, I was chatting to a lady and she told me about her life. **(b)** She had worked as a swimming teacher and I realised that she had worked in the school that my parents attended. I was surprised as I had heard her name being mentioned and now this lady did not look like she was capable of doing a job, let alone a physical job. This helped me to realise that the elderly people did have past experiences and some of them may have had important jobs. **(c)**

Assessor report: The learner has demonstrated some good understanding based on their own observations of how the care values have been put into place in two health and social care contexts **(b)**. However, there is still more of a focus on the care home than on the day nursery. The learner could provide more examples of activities they have completed themselves, which would back up their knowledge of how the care values are put into place. The learner should also be cautious about bringing personal connections into a piece of written work. The learner has obviously gone to a setting in their local area and has met a person that taught their parents. It is very good that they have made the connection that elderly residents have had past experiences which were important to the local community **(c)**. However, the way this is written could be construed as gossip. The learner could have linked this finding to the care value of adopting a non-judgemental approach to practice.

Reflective log

At both placements, as well as showing my CRB check and photographic identification before I was admitted, I was also asked to ensure that I signed in and out of the building every day. The secretary of the school explained to me that this was part of their safeguarding policy. Whilst I was attending the care home I witnessed more safeguarding values being put into place: while the care workers were helping the service users with everyday tasks, they also ensured that their physical and emotional well-being was sustained.

There was a meeting about one resident whilst I was in placement. There was personal information in this meeting and I was not permitted to attend. I was asked to go into the day room with another care worker and play games or chat to the residents. This was when I was chatting to the lady who told me about her past career as a swimming teacher. I realised that just because these people are now slowing down and have become disengaged with some of their usual activities, they still had busy lives and important jobs in their past. This helped me to realise that we should not be judgemental. I also noticed that all of the care workers spoke to the residents on an individual basis, ensuring that they treated them as individuals. This helped to maintain their self-esteem and is an example of the care value of respect for the individual.

Whilst I was attending the care home I was reminded that if I did gather any information about the resident, then it should remain confidential and that they were presuming that I would follow their codes of conduct. This would involve not gossiping outside of the setting. I realised that this was another care value being put into place, and I felt very proud that I was being treated like a professional.

Having key workers on every shift for each resident ensured that every individual's needs were being fully met in a person-centred way, as the care workers had built up a very good relationship with the service users built upon trust and respect. They were not judgemental and also involved the service users in decisions about their care. Some service users took the lead in this interaction and made choices for themselves such as what they were going to wear that day. As I was not a permanent member of the working team, I was asked to go out of the room when personal care, such as washing and changing, was taking place. This was to maintain the service user's dignity, which is another care value.

I also was asked to help hand out the meals on several occasions. This is when I noticed that not everyone was given the same meal; there was a choice and the service user could choose what they would like from the menu the day before. There were several dietary requirements met within the meals, for instance, one man had coeliac disease and therefore he had a gluten-free meal provided and two other service users had different meals due to religious beliefs.

I learnt a lot whilst I was on placement and observed the use of care values in both a care home for the elderly and a day care facility for children.

Assessor report: The learner has provided further examples of activities they have completed themselves, which back up their knowledge of how the care values are put into place. However, they have still focused on the care home and have not demonstrated the use of care values in the day care facility.

Assessor report – overall

The learner has demonstrated the care values required to work within the health and social care sector in great depth. However, her account is heavily reliant on only one type of setting. Although the learner has indicated that they attended two settings, they have not demonstrated how the values were used with different service user groups.

Is the evidence sufficient to satisfy the grading criteria?

Not fully as the criteria asks for a demonstration of the use of values in selected health and social care contexts, and this learner's response is heavily reliant on only one context.

What could be improved?

The learner should demonstrate more use of the care values in the second placement. This would show how these values are used in different contexts with different service users; it would also give an opportunity to go into more depth about some of the values, such as safeguarding.

(2A.M1) Discuss the importance of the values that underpin current practice in health and social care, with reference to specific examples.

Assessor report: This criterion can be achieved by building upon the evidence the learner provided for 2A.P1, or answered as a separate piece of work. The command word is **discuss**. In order to achieve this, the learner should provide thoughtful and logical arguments to support why the values that underpin current practice are important.

✎ Learner answer

Values that are used in health and social care are very important. For example, confidentiality is important in keeping individuals' information private and on a need-to-know basis. It is important to preserve the dignity and respect of individuals when providing care for them. Safeguarding is another important value to ensure that users of health and social care are not neglected. It is also important to use a person-centred approach when delivering care to individuals.

Assessor report: The learner has correctly identified most of the values that underpin current practice in health and social care. However, the learner now needs to develop their answer by discussing further why these values are important, and include specific examples that relate to health and social care settings. To achieve 2A.M1, the learner must provide at least one example of each of the key values. These examples can be of good or bad practice.

Learner answer

Care values within health and social care settings are very important to both the service user and the health and social care worker. For example, within a day nursery setting, all of the children's personal details will be held in a locked filing cabinet or on a password-protected computer. **(a)** This ensures that the children are kept safe and that strangers do not get hold of their address or other personal details.

Another example is ensuring that health and social care workers are treating the service user with dignity and respect. This can be observed in a care home for the elderly. Care workers will ensure that each individual resident's individual needs regarding care and well-being are met. For example, if a resident needed a particular diet then this would be provided. **(a)**

Safeguarding is also an important care value, especially when working with children in an after-school club. All staff and visitors should have completed a police (Criminal Records Bureau) check and they should sign in and out. **(a)**

The final care value to be discussed is using a person-centred approach to delivering care. In a residential setting for adults with learning difficulties, the health and social care workers will involve the service users when they are creating their care plan. They may involve them in decisions such as which activities they like to take part in and what their favourite meal is. **(a)**

Assessor report: The learner has correctly identified values that underpin current practice in health and social care, and has given some good examples relating to a range of health and social care settings **(a)**. However, this answer still lacks the discussion element of the criteria. In order to discuss, the learner should provide thoughtful and logical arguments to support their work.

It is important that the care values within health and social care settings are put into place. This benefits both the service user and the health and social care worker. If these care values were not put into place, then the physical and emotional well-being of individuals would suffer and there would not be trust and respect between the service user and the worker.

For example, within a day nursery setting for young children, all of the care values should be put into place to ensure all of the children's needs are being met. Confidentiality is one such value, therefore all of the children's personal details should be held in a locked filing cabinet which is stored in a staff area, or on a password-protected computer. This ensures that the children are kept safe and that only staff who need to know details have access to them and that strangers do not get hold of their personal records. If personal records were to get into the wrong hands, then the children's personal safety could be at risk. It would also cause mistrust from parents and give the setting a bad reputation. In some instances not keeping personal details safe can lead to gossip and emotional upset. Staff should remain professional at all times; they should make sure that any meetings or discussions held about the children are carried out in an appropriate place.

Another example will be ensuring that the health and social care worker is treating the service user with dignity and respect. This can be observed in a care home. Care professionals will make sure that each resident's individual needs regarding care and well-being are met. For example, if a resident needed a particular diet then this would be provided. If individuals' well-being was not taken into account then the service user's health and emotional well-being would be threatened. Another way that respect can be shown for the individual is ensuring that a non-judgemental approach is used within the setting.

Safeguarding is also an important care value, especially when working with children in an after-school club. All staff and visitors should have completed a Police (Criminal Records Bureau) check and sign in and out. If strangers are allowed to make contact with children then this could again be a safety risk. It is important that people working with children are qualified and have completed the safety checks required by law.

Assessor report: The learner has put much thought into the answer and demonstrated an understanding of most of the care values as related to health and social care settings. Some good creative examples have been used throughout, which partly address the criteria. The discussion of the importance of confidentiality is very good, but discussion of subsequent values lacks the same amount of depth. The learner has not included any discussion of the importance of a person-centred approach to care.

Assessor report – overall

Is the evidence sufficient to satisfy the grading criteria?

Not fully. The discussion element of the criteria is weak. It has been developed for some elements of the final answer but does not run through all of the answer.

What could be improved?

The learner should ensure that they understand all of the elements of the assessment criteria, and that they complete all of the parts of the answer to the same depth.

Assess the potential impact on the individual of effective and ineffective application of the care values in health and social care practice with reference to selected examples.

Assessor report: To achieve this criterion, the learner can build upon their evidence for 2A.M1, using the same examples and using the same health and social care settings. The command word in this criterion is **assess**. This means to give careful consideration to all factors that apply and identify which are the most important, with reasons.

✍ Learner answer

Care values can have an impact on individuals. For instance, if confidentiality was not followed correctly in a day nursery for children, then the children's personal safety could be at risk. Children should also be safeguarded in an after-school club. If the correct staff are not working with children then this can lead to the children's emotional needs not being understood. A person-centred approach should be used when working with adults who have learning difficulties; this will ensure that the service user will feel accepted and reassured, that they will be listened to and their needs will be met.

Assessor report: The learner has highlighted some of the potential impacts of effective application of care values on individual service users. However, their answer currently lacks depth. There is an awareness of how values will impact on the individual, but not all values that are listed in the unit content are included. There is some linking to practical settings, but the assessment element of the criterion is weak. To achieve 2A.D1, the learner should also consider some examples of ineffective application. Considering both effective and ineffective applications of all the care values and in a range of settings will allow them to make an assessment.

Learner answer

In a day nursery, if health and social care workers are effective in maintaining confidentiality then service users and their families will feel reassured and will trust and respect the setting, knowing that their personal details are safe. If confidentiality was not upheld correctly in a day nursery for children then the children's personal safety could be at risk. **(a)**

If dignity is maintained within a residential setting for the elderly, through appropriate actions, then all service users will be treated with respect and they will feel reassured in their environment. As a result their emotional well-being and self-esteem will be positive. If service users are not treated with dignity, this can lead to a feeling of loneliness and they may become isolated. **(a)**

Children should also be safeguarded in an after-school club. If the correct staff are not working with children then this can lead to the children's emotional needs not being understood. **(a)** When safeguarding is successfully in place then children should feel a sense of security.

A person-centred approach should be used when working with adults who have learning difficulties; this will ensure that the service user will feel accepted and reassured that they will be listened to and their needs will be met. If they do not feel they have been listened to this could result in an individual becoming withdrawn.

Assessor report: The learner has now demonstrated more depth in their answer. They have included some examples of the impact of ineffective application of care values **(a)**. There is still not a full assessment of the impact that effective and ineffective application of care values can have on individual service users. The learner should consider more how an individual's overall well-being can be affected by effective or ineffective practice in relation to the care values being put into place. All of the values within the unit content should be assessed.

Care values can have an impact on individuals in a range of different health and social care settings. Confidentiality in a day nursery can have a large impact on an individual's well-being. If health and social care workers were effective in maintaining confidentiality, through protecting personal data, not gossiping and ensuring that they held professional discussions in appropriate places then this would have a positive impact, as service users and their families will feel reassured and trust and respect the setting, knowing that their personal details are safe. If confidentiality was not upheld, and the health and social care workers were ineffective in carrying out this care value, then it would have a negative effect in many ways. One such impact could be that the children's personal safety could be at risk if their personal information was to get into the wrong hands. This could affect the child's feeling of security within the setting and the families' trust in professionals that they are leaving their children in the care of. This can also impact on self-esteem, especially if the parents or guardians of the children think that their personal details have been discussed with people that they did not wish their details to be discussed with. For the care values to have a positive impact on the individual, confidentiality must be upheld in a professional way, through professional codes of practice. This will maintain a professional, trusting relationship with service users and the health and social care workers.

Dignity should be maintained within a residential setting for the elderly through appropriate actions. If this carried out then all service users will be treated with respect, they will feel reassured in their environment and their emotional well-being and self-esteem will be positive. If service users are not treated with dignity, this can lead to a feeling of loneliness and they may become isolated. Dignity should be put into place to take into account the thoughts and feelings of the individual, especially when personal care is taking place. Using key workers can help maintain dignity, especially if intimate care practice is taking place. This way a trust bond can be built up between the care worker and the service user, which will put the service user at ease and help them to feel comfortable with the familiarity of their key person. If every day a different person were to carry out personal care then the service user may feel devalued and not worthy of individual attention. This can have a negative impact on an individual's physical and emotional well-being.

A person-centred approach should be used when working with adults who have learning difficulties. This will ensure that the service user feels accepted and reassured that they will be listened to and their needs will be met. If they do not feel they have been listened to this could result in an individual becoming withdrawn. An example of this is for the health and social care worker to get to know the individuals and their personal preferences, likes and dislikes. It is important that individuals with learning difficulties feel a sense of control and independence in their lives; this will raise their self-esteem and in turn make them feel valued. If a service user with learning difficulties is not understood and made to do activities that they dislike, or to eat something that they dislike, this could have a negative impact on the individual. It could make them feel sad and frustrated, cause them to display unwanted behaviour, or make them refuse to join in. This in turn could have an effect on the other service users and carers.

It is important, therefore, that each care value is put into place effectively to have a positive impact on the individual.

Assessor report: The learner has carried out some assessment of some of the care values. They have considered a range of factors that could impact on an individual in terms of effective or ineffective delivery of the care values in a range of settings. However, not all of the care values included in the unit content have been addressed.

Assessor report – overall

Is the evidence sufficient to satisfy the grading criterion?

Not fully. Not all of the care values that are in the unit content have been assessed.

What could be improved?

The learner should ensure that they cover all of the care values that are listed in the unit content.

Learning aim B

Investigate ways of empowering individuals who use health and social care services

Learning aim B provides you with the opportunity to understand the application of the methods that are implemented to empower individuals. Individuals can access care in many settings, including care homes, day centres, hospitals and health centres.

Assessment criteria

2B.P3	Describe ways in which care workers can empower individuals, using relevant examples from health and social care.
2B.P4	Explain why it is important to take individual circumstances into account when planning care that will empower an individual, using relevant examples from health and social care.
2B.M2	Discuss the extent to which individual circumstances can be taken into account when planning care that will empower them, using relevant examples from health and social care.
2B.D2	Assess the potential difficulties in taking individual circumstances into account when planning care that will empower an individual, making suggestions for improvement.

Topic B.1 Empowering individuals

In the past few years there have been several changes in how individuals who use health and social services are consulted and in how they can be more involved in decision making. This makes the individual the focus and provides them with the opportunity to be more involved in their treatment and care. Empowering an individual will give them a feeling of strength and control over their life.

Everyone is different but there are some issues that are important to everybody, including wanting to feel that they belong, being given choices and the opportunity to make decisions, being treated as an individual and being given respect.

Adapting activities and environments

Studied

All individuals should have the opportunity to participate in the same activities as everyone else, whether they are daily routines, chores or hobbies. Everyone should have the opportunity to participate in social interaction, building relationships and developing their skills and interests. Providing the opportunity to participate in an activity that satisfies a physical need will often satisfy other needs. For example, a trip to the supermarket improves mobility (a physical need) but will also include social interaction and help build confidence (emotional needs). An individual may need support to participate in an activity; the level of support should never be assumed but should be matched to the need of the individual. The type of support and guidance and the timescale over which it is given will vary from individual to individual.

Figure 2.6 A trip to the supermarket improves mobility and builds confidence

It may take time to plan an activity that is not part of a daily routine, but plans should take into consideration personal choice and preferences. An activity may require changes to the environment so that it remains safe for different individuals but accessing the activity will encourage independence.

It is important that the individual is consulted in the activities they want to undertake and the support they will need. Participating in activities will help an individual keep physically fit and alert, promote self-image and self-esteem, interact socially with others, develop skills and interests and become more confident. Achievement in any activity should be acknowledged by praise and encouragement as this will boost an individual's confidence and self-esteem.

Individual rights, preferences and needs

Studied

People can often be stereotyped by the way they look or dress, and assumptions can easily be made about what they need. Anyone accessing health and social care services should be treated equally, with dignity and respect, regardless of their class, gender, race, religion, age or disability.

A positive effect on building self-image and self-esteem will involve making sure that an individual's basic needs, such as personal hygiene, food and warmth, are being met. Personal hygiene is important but people will have different preferences: some may like to shower and others will prefer a bath; some may only like to use certain brands of shampoo or soap. Individuals should be provided with the opportunity to keep to their routine for personal hygiene and for an individual this may be important for religious beliefs. For example, Muslims need to be able to wash their hands in running water and Hindus will prefer a shower to a bath. Self-image plays an important role in building confidence and an individual should be encouraged to follow personal preference on how they dress and style their hair.

To achieve a balanced diet, an individual should be provided with the opportunity to have a variety of foods, but everyone will have foods they like or dislike. Also, when food is prepared for individuals from different religions it is important to ensure these people are not offered food they avoid for religious reasons. For example, Hindus do not eat beef; Jews and Muslims do not eat pork.

Although everyone is different with different behaviours and preferences, we all have a similar range of emotions. Treating an individual as unique and being non-judgemental about their behaviour and preferences will make them feel confident that their needs are recognised.

Difficulties in accessing care

Studied

Most people will have no problems in accessing the health and social care services they need, but some may encounter problems such as accessing information or getting to the relevant venue. An individual may not be able to read or understand the information that is available and may be reluctant to ask for support. An individual will want to be independent but may not be able to access the health and care services without supported transport.

An activity will need to be assessed for each individual; the activity may be perfectly safe for one person but a hazard for another. The activity may need adjusting to make it safe and accessible for different individuals. Physical limitations, such as pain in joints or swelling, may impact on an individual undertaking some activities. To prevent further injury or damage, it may be necessary to make adjustments to equipment or activities. Activities should be matched to the needs of the individual. For example, an individual may feel angry or annoyed if the activity is not helping them and they feel that no progress has been made.

When working with a group where there is a mix of different cultures it may be difficult to implement activities that meet the needs of everyone. The timetable of activities should be varied and made available for the group so they can choose the ones they like.

The availability of resources may impact on the choices available for an individual. Some social activities require very few resources but others may require specialist support staff and expensive equipment.

A health and social care provider may encounter times when they feel that the individual has made choices and decisions that are not the most appropriate – for example, an individual who refuses to continue to take medication they need. The health and social care provider has a duty of care and will need to seek support from managers or other professionals.

A willingness to work with others

Studied

To maintain and sustain their lifestyle, an individual may need to involve others such as family, friends or staff from health and social care services. For the transition to work effectively, the individual and those providing the support will need cooperation and commitment.

Recovering from an illness or an accident may leave an individual feeling weak but they will want to establish their independence as soon as possible. Previously, health and social care providers have had the responsibility for deciding the care and treatment required for individuals. Today individuals are being involved in discussing and choosing their care and treatments; this has been proven to help the individual emotionally and to accelerate independence. Following an accident or a stay in hospital or in care facilities, an individual may find returning home daunting. Maintaining personal hygiene, daily routines and chores may be difficult and the individual may need to depend on care and support.

An individual may require health and social care support from several different departments or organisations, who will work in a team or partnership to meet the needs of the individual. Each member of the team will need an understanding of the roles of the other members of the partnership and to implement effective communication channels. For the service to be effective, the individual will have to take responsibility for keeping appointments and being at home for planned visits.

Figure 2.7 Team working

People who are ill will often want to stay at home so that they are near family and friends. Although an individual might depend on family and friends for practical support, they will also be responsible for providing emotional support by making the individual feel safe and secure. Family and friends provide the social interaction that will prevent the individual from feeling isolated or lonely. Family and friends are usually very willing to provide support but may have other commitments such as children or employment.

Promoting choice

Studied ☐

An individual should be encouraged to make choices about the treatment, care and the support they receive. There could be a time when the health or social care provider feels that an individual would benefit from a different type of activity or treatment but the individual may be reluctant to try anything different. Continual talk or discussion on the proposed changes may result in the individual feeling bullied and this will impact on the relationship between the individual and the health and social care provider. The care worker could review other strategies to help the individual understand the benefits of change but any changes must be ultimately made by the individual.

Involving an individual in making decisions about their care and treatment will impact on their attitude to any planned treatment or activities. The activities will be more effective if they are the individual's own choice and reflect their interests.

Preferred methods of communication

Studied ☐

Communication is an important tool and is necessary in asking for and providing information, to identify choice and express needs and feelings. Verbal communication is often seen as the main way to communicate, but the use of written communication, body language and gestures can also communicate messages. Written communication can be a formal letter or instructions on care or just a short note. Nodding or shaking the head can be used in response to questions and gestures such shaking a fist can be seen as anger. However, care should be taken when using body language or gestures as these can be interpreted differently by different cultures or races. For example, in many cultures, eye contact is encouraged to show active listening but in Asian and Middle Eastern countries, eye contact is seen as being disrespectful.

Communication and active listening is important, not just for getting information but in building a relationship and trust. It is important that individuals are provided with the opportunity to use their preferred method of communication and that they are treated with dignity, respect and courtesy.

Different languages are often seen as a barrier to communication but with time and patience the barriers can be removed. Individuals should be given the choice to speak in their first language where English is an additional language. If an interpreter is used, it is important to speak to the individual and not the interpreter. Most misunderstandings can be avoided by speaking more slowly, asking for clarification, regularly checking understanding and refraining from using jargon.

If an individual has a speech impairment, time and patience are important. When you do not understand the information you are being given by someone with a speech impairment it is correct to ask the individual to repeat what they said. Understanding can then be confirmed by repeating back what the individual has said.

If an individual has a hearing impairment, it is important to get their attention before starting a conversation and always look directly at the person. There is no need to shout, just speak in a normal tone of voice using short, simple sentences. If a sign language interpreter is needed, any communication should be addressed to the individual and not the interpreter. Makaton is a combination of picture symbols, hand gestures and is a language used by adults and children with learning disabilities and communication problems. The aim of Makaton is to help people communicate through speech and when the user is able to say the correct words, then they are encouraged to speak rather than sign.

If the individual is in a wheelchair, communication can be more effective if the speaker is at eye level with the individual. The speaker should ensure that they are never patronising, condescending or childish.

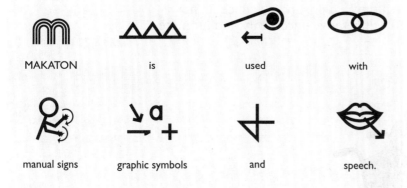

MAKATON   is   used   with

manual signs   graphic symbols   and   speech.

Figure 2.8 Makaton

Reasons for supporting individuals

People who are employed in a health and social care role are working with individuals to improve their independence and self-esteem and to promote their individuality and overall well-being. An individual should be encouraged and supported to live as independently as possible.

When an individual is recovering from an illness or accident, they will be reliant on health and social care providers, but for their self-esteem and well-being it is important to encourage some independence as soon as possible. This will involve helping the individual to make the choices that will make them as independent as they want. When an individual is struggling with a daily task, it is easier to take over, but to promote independence the task should be completed with them. It is important to organise any support around the needs of the individual and agree with them when help will be required and the level and type of support required. With the individual deciding on the level of support, this will encourage them to succeed and be more independent.

An individual may need support in accessing relevant information or in learning how to use equipment. Accessing information could provide guidance on how to improve their lifestyle and help them make choices for the future. Advice and guidance on how to use new equipment will help remove uncertainty and promote confidence.

Figure 2.9 Information should be accessible

Personal identity is what makes an individual unique; it is a mix of their appearance, culture, background and characteristics. Personal identity is linked to self-image, how an individual will think and feel about themselves and how they imagine other people see them. An individual with a low self-image will have low self-esteem and this will impact on how they interact with others, including health and social care providers. Self-image and

UNIT 2 Health and Social Care Values

self-esteem have an impact on well-being. To provide support and encouragement for an individual's well-being, a health and social care provider will need to know what is important to that individual. For one individual, well-being may be feeling fine and free from illness and for another, well-being could be feeling valued by others and having a purpose for living.

Promoting autonomy

Studied ▢

Autonomy is the right of an individual to make decisions and choices about their medical care and treatment without the health care provider trying to influence the decision.

Promoting autonomy for an individual using health and social care services is helping them to become independent and to do things for themselves. There will be many situations when a health or social care provider will want to take over an activity that the individual is finding difficult or taking too long to complete. For example, it may take an individual longer to get themselves dressed, a task which would take their carer a few minutes. Allowing the individual to dress themselves encourages independence. Individuals who have been ill or who are recovering from an accident may have become dependent on the care service and will need to be encouraged to do things for themselves. The individual should be provided with regular, positive, encouraging feedback on their accomplishments and this will give them the confidence to build on what they have achieved.

When using new equipment or trying new activities, it is important for the individual to receive reassurance and encouragement. Trying new activities will help the individual retain their existing skills but also develop new skills and improve independence.

Getting to know the individual and what is important to them will help to build their trust. Consistency in behaviour and providing the individual with accurate information about their treatment and progress will also help in building their trust.

Communicating effectively with an individual is important so that their choices and wishes can be established and consent given for any care or treatment. When an individual is unable to provide their consent, either verbally, by signing language or in writing, then an **advocate** will be appointed. The advocate is someone who tries to understand the needs and wishes of the individual and will speak on their behalf.

Use of positive working practices

When an individual is facing changes, especially in their accommodation, it is important that relevant care and support are implemented. The needs of the individual for managing everyday tasks will be assessed before any plan can be developed. The assessment, which may involve different professionals, will identify the abilities and needs of the individual. The plan will outline the activities required to meet the needs of an individual. The plan will include targets that can be monitored. For example, the plan for an individual who needs to improve mobility may involve progressing from a wheelchair to using walking sticks. The plan will only be effective if the individual is committed to it and this can be achieved by the individual being involved in making the decisions. Monitoring and recording the progress made can identify when and if adjustments or modifications are required. It is important that the individual is involved in any discussion about their progress and changes.

Anyone accessing health and care services should be treated as an individual and this incudes understanding their culture, their beliefs and values. To avoid making assumptions about an individual's values, a health and social care provider should take time to get to know the individual. Valuing diversity means that no group or individual is treated as being superior to another and that everyone has equal access to opportunities and activities.

Figure 2.10 Valuing diversity

A risk assessment is essential before any activity occurs and may highlight obstacles that need to be considered in order for the plan to be successful. A risk assessment will identify potential hazards and, once identified, processes can be implemented to remove the hazard or minimise any risks of harm. There may be times when an individual wants to participate in an activity that is not free from risks. To be effective and to avoid disappointment, the risk assessment, whenever possible, should be implemented during the early planning stage.

UNIT 2 Health and Social Care Values

Knowledge recap questions

1. Thespian Lass is a care home for retired stage performers. Why should the care home encourage the empowering of its staff when they deal with clients?

2. Sue, a patient, doesn't want to be bathed by any of the male staff. Why should the supervisor try to accommodate this request?

3. What is Makaton?

4. The owners of the care home have given the supervisor 'complete autonomy' in how she runs the staff timetable and the menus. What benefits will this bring?

5. Why does the care home carry out a risk assessment on every new resident?

Assessment guidance for Learning aim B

2B.P3 **Describe ways in which care workers can empower individuals, using relevant examples from health and social care.**

Assessor report: The command word for 2B.P3 is **describe**. To achieve this, the learner will need to give a clear description that includes all of the relevant ways in which care workers can empower individuals. They should include examples from health and social care settings; this may include basing their evidence on case studies of service users.

✍ Learner answer

Care workers can empower service users by applying the care values of health and social care in order to meet the needs of the individual they are caring for. The care worker should make sure the service user feels respected in the setting. In a hospital, for example, it is important that the nurse can communicate effectively with their patient. If he/she does not know the patient's preferred method of communication then they can look at the care plan, where this information should be recorded. If a patient's first language is not English then a translator could be provided and written information in their first language given. By taking the time to do this, the nurse is showing the patient that they are valued and is taking into account their preferences and needs. This will empower them as it will make them feel valued and respected and promote their independence and well-being. By using positive working practices the service user will feel valued; this can build trust in the professionals, thereby promoting a supportive and empowering relationship.

Assessor report: The learner has provided an example of ways in which the care worker can empower service users in one setting (a hospital), Although this example is relevant, the work could be improved by the use of further examples from various settings and including how settings meet the physical, intellectual, emotional and social needs of the user. There are also limited examples of practice which promotes the individual's autonomy. The answer could have been expanded to show how preferred methods of communication could be utilised to build a trusting relationship and promote individuality. The learner shows understanding of the promotion of empowerment in the hospital setting by mentioning the use of a preferred method of communication, but this could have been extended to include other types of communication, e.g. Makaton. The learner could include a description of the care-planning process and the importance of including service users, their family and relevant professionals, as well as the difficulties that workers experience in taking individual circumstances into account when planning care.

Care workers can also empower service users by using good practice and applying the care values of health and social care in order to meet physical, intellectual, emotional and social needs. In a day care setting, for example, care workers should provide activities that meet the individual needs of the service user and support them to participate fully, even if this means that the activity needs to be changed so that those who want to participate can. For example, if someone is in a wheelchair the care setting can provide a risk assessment and identify on the care plan any adaptations that are needed in the environment to promote dignity and respect for the individual and empower them to take part in their chosen activity. **(a)**

A GP can use effective communication to make sure they are recognising their patient's individual rights and can promote choice when giving care. They can also ensure the patient has an advocate if they feel it is necessary to support the patient in planning any treatment. **(b)**

If a service user is returning home after a hospital stay in which they are recovering from a stroke, a social worker would develop a care plan that would include the client's needs and preferences. These needs would be part of the needs-led assessment. Other professionals such as a physiotherapist and occupational therapist could be involved in assessing and treating the service user. **(c)** The care worker could promote empowerment by supporting the service user in their own house: hand rails could be fitted which will help the service user in daily living and promote autonomy. This will enhance the service user's quality of life, providing support as needed but promoting individuality and the overall well-being of the service user, by giving choice as to the level of support required.

Assessor report: The learner has provided examples of ways in which the care worker can empower service users, with examples of practice that promote the individual's autonomy. Care planning could have been described, with reference to the importance of ensuring that the service user and family are included in this process **(b)**. The learner has also described working with others in partnership **(c)**.

A good example is given of how the environment can be adapted to include a service user in a wheelchair **(a)**, but it should be remembered that not all adaptations need to be physical ones; for example, some service users may need social support to participate in activities. The learner could expand the work by including more settings and how workers may meet the physical, intellectual, emotional and social well-being of the client.

Assessor report – overall

What is good about this assessment evidence?

The learner has provided some good examples of ways in which the care worker can empower service users in a variety of settings. The examples are relevant and demonstrate the learner's understanding of practices that can promote empowerment.

What could be improved?

This work could have been improved with more description of the importance of including family members as well as the service user in the care planning process, and the difficulties that workers experience in taking individual circumstances into account when planning care. Although the learner has identified examples of service user empowerment in a variety of settings, they could have used these to describe how intellectual, emotional and social needs could be met.

2B.P4 Explain why it is important to take individual circumstances into account when planning care that will empower an individual, using relevant examples from health and social care.

Assessor report: The command word for this criterion is explain. To do this, the learner will need to set out in detail, with reasons, why it is important to take individual circumstances into account when planning care that will empower an individual. They should include examples from health and social care that are relevant.

✍ Learner answer

The care worker should identify the individual circumstances of the service user. This is important in order to empower the service user. It is important to take into account their needs and preferences. However, in some circumstances this can be difficult.

Multi-disciplinary team work can mean that the service user's individual circumstances can be considered and their care planned to address their needs. Care workers work hard to support individuals, to promote independence and empower the service user, considering individual needs and choice, as this can promote overall well-being. This means that the care worker must put the individual's preference at the centre of planning. For example, even if they may think that the best option is residential care, but the service user would like to remain in their own home, it is important that the care worker recognises the rights of the individual to make choices about their care and empowers the individual to stay at home. (a)

Assessor report: The learner has identified the importance of taking into account the individual's circumstances, but they need to demonstrate their understanding by providing examples of how the care workers could do this and why it is important to the service user and the care planning process. The example of the service user wanting to remain in their own home **(a)** is good, but could be extended to explain the factors that would need to be considered, such as taking the service user's desires into account and balancing needs and rights with safety.

✍ Learner answer

Identifying the individual circumstances of the service user is important as without knowing individual circumstances, the care worker cannot provide client-centred care. In order to empower the service user it is important to take into account their needs and preferences and put the service user at the centre of any care planning. This can be difficult in some circumstances. For example, when a service user has had a number of accidents in their own home involving falls and, despite support such as hand rails and personal carers being provided, the service user continues to fall. Their care plan may have to be reviewed and this must include a risk assessment, which would identify the fact that it is not safe for the service user to live in their own home, despite support and the fact that this is their choice. **(b)**

It is important that the care worker recognises the rights of the individual to make choices about their care. To ensure empowerment of the individual, if it is safe and feasible for the service user to stay at home then this should be considered and appropriate support put in place.

Assessor report: The learner has provided some good examples of ways in which the care worker can empower service users, whilst considering individual circumstances **(b)**. Their answer could be improved by recognising the rights of the individual to make their own choices and the benefits of a needs-led assessment that identifies the individual needs of the service user. The learner could also explain the need to build a trusting relationship and encourage feedback from the client, which they could also provide examples of. The learner could expand an explanation of the difficulties that can be experienced while trying to provide client-centred care and empowering the service user, for example, service-led assessment. Although the idea of multi-disciplinary working is identified in the first part of their answer, this could be expanded here to explain the benefits to the service user. Further examples would also be useful in demonstrating their understanding, as would an explanation of the importance of making the service user feel valued.

Putting the service user at the centre of any care planning can be difficult. The best care would be needs-led care, but sometimes there are not the appropriate services or resources available and it becomes service-led assessment. For example, if a service user would benefit from specialised treatment but funding for this is not available in their area, then this need cannot be met and an alternative treatment plan could be offered. However, this may result in the service user feeling less valued.

It is important that the care worker recognises the rights of the individual to make their own choices in order to build a trusting relationship which will encourage feedback from the client. For the individual who has had a series of accidents and for whom risk assessment has identified that it is no longer safe for them to live in their own home despite this being their choice, this can be difficult. The care worker would be responsible for ensuring the service user's safety in their home and because of this, the best option may be residential care. In this case it would be very important to encourage the family to become involved in the care-planning process as this would help support the service user and look at possible other options that would meet the needs of the service user and still promote choice and autonomy.

To ensure empowerment of the individual, if it is safe and feasible for the service user to stay at home then this should be considered and appropriate support put in place. For example, an occupational therapist could do a home assessment to ensure the environment is adapted and meets the specific needs of the service user, to promote their autonomy and empowerment. In this way, the service user will feel valued and respected and will preserve autonomy over their well-being.

Assessor report – overall

What is good about this assessment evidence?

The learner has provided some good examples of ways in which the care worker can empower service whilst considering individual circumstances. The examples are relevant and demonstrate the learner's understanding of practices that can promote empowerment and they have also included examples of individual circumstances and how this may impact on planning the care. Risk assessment has also been considered when considering individual circumstances.

What could be improved?

The work could be improved by giving specific examples of how all areas of the client's needs can be met to promote empowerment.

(2B.M2) **Discuss the extent to which individual circumstances can be taken into account when planning care that will empower them, using relevant examples from health and social care.**

Assessor report: The command word for this criterion is **discuss**. To achieve this, the learner will need to consider the different aspects of individual circumstances when planning care that will empower the individual, how they interrelate and the extent to which they are important. They should include relevant examples from health and social care.

✎ **Learner answer**

It is important to take individual circumstances into account in the care planning process. However, if the setting is meeting the needs of many service users, it can be difficult to balance the rights of all of them. At all times the individual circumstances of each service user should be taken into account when planning care. Unfortunately, this cannot always be provided due to limited resources, funding issues and lack of services in health and social care provision.

Assessor report: The learner has identified that it is important to take into account individual circumstances, but has not demonstrated an understanding of the extent to which these circumstances can be accommodated and the factors that influence this when planning care. The learner should give examples from a variety of health and social care settings, which will provide the opportunity to discuss the difficulties of always taking individual circumstances into account.

Although the learner has identified that limited resources, services and funding can make it difficult to provide needs-led assessment and care, they have not included a discussion of this, with examples, to support their ideas.

To develop the answer further the learner should discuss limited resources, services and training and the impact this has on needs-led assessment and care. The service user's likes and preferences should be taken into account and difficulties discussed.

✍ Learner answer

Taking individual circumstances into account in the care planning process is not always possible. It can be difficult to balance the rights of all service users. Although we know that needs-led assessment and care makes service users feel valued and promotes their empowerment, as care workers we may need to provide a service-led care package. If a service user had to go into a nursing home and had special dietary needs related to their religion, this may sometimes be difficult to provide due to cost, availability and staff training. Provision provided may not necessarily be as close to the family home as the service user might like, resulting in extra travelling for family members to visit. As a result the service user may feel lonely and not valued and lack empowerment.

Assessor report: The learner has provided limited discussion of the extent to which individual circumstances should be taken into account. The learner has provided one example. To improve this work the learner should expand their discussion to include more examples from different health and social care settings and also discuss why it is important to take account of individual circumstances when planning and providing care.

It is not always possible to take into account individual circumstances because of finances, available resources and services. As care workers we may need to provide a service-led care package because the services needed are not available or because funding is limited and the waiting list for some services can be long.

If a service user has a stroke and wanted to return to the family home and their partner was unable to care for them, then the service user may need a care plan put in place. This could include adaptations to their home and perhaps support workers visiting three times a day. This process can be time consuming and difficult to put in place as the family home may be difficult to adapt. This may mean that the service user may need to move house, which can take time and may result in them having to move into residential care as a temporary solution. Also funding may not be available for three daily visits by support workers and therefore family members may need to provide care. If the service user was a man who needed personal care, he may want a male carer to provide this. If only female carers were available then this would mean that their choice could not be respected.

A day care centre may be limited in the activities they can provide due to budget, staffing levels and staff skills. Service users may have various interests and meeting all of these choices can be very difficult. As a consequence some service users may feel like their needs are not being met, so they may feel less empowered as their interests are not being addressed. For example, if the majority of the service users would like bingo and a small minority would like a book club, limited staffing and resources may mean that only the bingo could be offered.

Assessor report – overall

What is good about this assessment evidence?

The learner has discussed the extent to which individual circumstances can be considered when planning care that empowers the individual. This is supported with some good examples that demonstrate an understanding of the difficulties of always providing needs-led assessment and care. The learner has discussed limited resources, services and training and also identified the need for service users' likes and preferences to be taken into account and the difficulties that care workers may experience.

What could be improved?

The work could be improved by looking at care planning as a two-way process that encourages effective communication and feedback with the service user and their family, as this will build a trusting relationship, promoting autonomy and empowerment for the individual by still providing choice.

Case study

Mr Fred Abrahams was diagnosed with Alzheimer's disease three years ago and he is progressively deteriorating. When Mr Abrahams is having a good day he begs his wife Mary not to leave him. Mary is struggling with his care and she is becoming very concerned about his safety as he has left the house on a number of occasions when she has been asleep. She is exhausted and her own health is starting to suffer as a result of his condition. This has resulted in their daughter Lucy staying over four nights a week so that her mother can rest. Lucy contacted social services as the whole family feel it is time for Fred to go into nursing care. Fred does not want to leave his own home.

Assessor report: The command word for this criterion is **assess**. To achieve this, the learner should make a judgement on the potential difficulties in taking individual circumstances into account when planning care that will empower the individual in relation to the case study provided. They should make suggestions for improvements to Mr Abrahams's care.

✍ Learner answer

There can be difficulties when taking service users' individual circumstances into account to plan their care. It is important to assess the needs of the service user. Communication can be difficult due to many factors and this can make planning care very difficult. **(a)** The difficulty in empowering a service user could be that the service user does not want to go into a nursing home. If a risk assessment has identified the safety of the service user is a concern in their own home, then nursing care may be the only option. **(b)** Another potential difficulty could be a lack of places in local nursing homes. **(c)**

Assessor report: The learner has identified that communication may be a potential difficulty when assessing the care needs of a service user **(a)** but they have not related their example to the case study which was provided. The learner should extend their work and use the case study to help identify potential difficulties and demonstrate their knowledge and understanding of how these potential difficulties could be overcome. They could, for example take into account the professionals who could support effective communication and ensure that rights are recognised. Although the learner has identified safety as a potential risk **(b)**, they could have extended their answer to suggest the benefit of risk assessment. The learner also identifies that places may not be available in local nursing homes **(c)**. Here, they could have suggested alternatives to improve the outcome and safety for the service user. There is little mention of the importance of empowering the service user when planning care and their physical, intellectual, emotional and social needs are not addressed. The learner should now use the case study to provide focus for their assessment of the potential difficulties in taking individual circumstances into account when planning care that ensures empowerment of the service user.

There are potential difficulties when taking Mr Abrahams's individual circumstances into account to plan his care. It is important to assess the needs of Mr Abrahams using effective communication. Communication with Mr Abrahams can be difficult due to his confusion as a result of the Alzheimer's; he may find communication with a variety of professionals difficult. Mary feels guilty but is exhausted and her own health is starting to suffer and she feels it is best for her husband to go into a nursing home.

The difficulty in empowering Mr Abrahams is in that he does not want to go into a nursing home. A risk assessment has identified that in order to keep Mr Abrahams safe and support his family, nursing care is really the only long-term option as his condition is deteriorating. **(d)** Nursing homes identified as suitable should preferably be within travelling distance for his family to visit regularly but this may be difficult if places are not available in his local area. **(e)**

Assessor report: The learner has identified that communication may be a potential difficulty when assessing the care needs of Mr Abrahams; again they could have extended the work to make suggestions of professionals that could support him in achieving effective communication and ensuring his rights are recognised. The learner has recognised the importance of a risk assessment **(d)**, which acknowledges Mr Abrahams's safety as an issue. Nursing care is recommended as the best option for Mr Abrahams. The learner has identified that places may not be available but has not developed their answer **(e)**. This could include alternative support to empower and promote the well-being of the service user and his family. The work could then be extended to include Mr Abrahams's physical, intellectual, emotional and social needs to allow further assessment of the potential difficulties in taking individual circumstances into account and supporting empowerment.

Learner answer

Initially it will be important to assess the needs of Mr Abrahams and this may be difficult as effective communication is at the centre of client-centred care. As a result of Mr Abrahams's Alzheimer's, he may need an advocate to support his right to make choices. Communication with a variety of professionals may add to Mr Abrahams's confusion and it may be best that the advocate attends meetings on his behalf and supports Mrs Abrahams. When the advocate communicates with the service user, he/she could keep their language simple and he/she may need to have the same conversation a number of times; this could also be supported with written information so that his wife could also discuss options with him.

The advocate and Mr Abrahams's family could take him on visits to the available nursing homes so he could be supported in making his own choice. It would be very useful to plan these visits to correspond with when Mr Abrahams is less confused. Nursing homes identified as suitable should preferably be within travelling distance for his family to visit regularly, but this may be difficult if places are not available in his local area. Support workers could be put in place to support Mr Abrahams's care until a suitable nursing home becomes available, but limited places may mean that this may take some time so the care plan will need to be reviewed and adapted as Mr Abraham's condition continues to advance.

Assessor report – overall

What is good about this assessment evidence?

The learner has successfully used the case study to identify and assess some of the potential difficulties in taking Mr Abrahams's circumstances into account when planning care that will empower him, including some suggestions for improvement.

What could be improved?

The work could be improved by looking at Mr Abrahams's needs in terms of physical, intellectual, emotional and social support, as this will allow further assessment of the potential difficulties in taking individual circumstances into account and supporting empowerment.

Sample assignment brief 1: Using care values to support service users

PROGRAMME NAME	BTEC Level 2 First Award in Health and Social Care
ASSIGNMENT TITLE	Using care values to support service users
ASSESSMENT EVIDENCE	Written reports for an information booklet

This assignment will assess the following learning aim and grading criteria:

Learning aim A: Explore the care values that underpin current practice in health and social care

2A.P1 Describe how care values support users of services, using relevant examples.

2A.P2 Demonstrate the use of care values in selected health and social care contexts.

2A.M1 Discuss the importance of the values that underpin current practice in health and social care, with reference to selected examples.

2A.D1 Assess the potential impact on the individual of effective and ineffective application of the care values in health and social care practice, with reference to selected examples.

Scenario

As a student in a residential care home you have been asked to produce an information booklet for new members of staff about how care values are used to support service users.

Task 1

(a) Write a description of how care values support service users using relevant examples.

(b) Discuss the importance of the values that underpin care with reference to the examples you gave in the previous section.

(c) Prepare an assessment of the potential impact on the individual of:

- effective application of care values in health and social care practice
- ineffective application of care values in health and social care practice.

Use examples to support your assessment in each case.

Task 2

Obtain a witness testimony to show you can demonstrate the use of all the care values in two health and social care settings.

(You may have to do this through simulation if work placement is not arranged.)

Sample assignment brief 2: Empowering individuals who use health and social care services

PROGRAMME NAME	BTEC Level 2 First Award in Health and Social Care
ASSIGNMENT TITLE	Empowering individuals who use health and social care services
ASSESSMENT EVIDENCE	Written reports for an information booklet

This assignment will assess the following learning aim and grading criteria:

Learning aim B: Investigate ways of empowering individuals who use health and social care services

2B.P3 Describe ways in which care workers can empower individuals, using relevant examples from health and social care.

2B.P4 Explain why it is important to take individual circumstances into account when planning care that will empower an individual, using relevant examples from health and social care.

2B.M2 Discuss the extent to which individual circumstances can be taken into account when planning care that will empower them, using relevant examples from health and social care.

2B.D2 Assess the potential difficulties in taking individual circumstances into account when planning care that will empower an individual, making suggestions for improvement.

Scenario

As a student in a residential care home you have been asked to produce an information booklet for new members of staff about how care values are used to support service users.

Task 1

(a) Describe ways in which care workers can empower individuals using relevant examples from health and social care.

(b) Include a section discussing the extent to which individual circumstances can be taken into account when planning care that will empower them, using relevant examples from health and social care.

(c) Assess the potential difficulties in taking individual circumstances into account when planning care that empowers individuals. Make suggestions for improvements to overcome the difficulties.

Task 2

Use a case study to describe how an individual's circumstances can be used to create a care plan that empowers them. Explain why it is important to take individual circumstances into account when planning such care. Include examples from a range of health and social care settings.

Unit 1 Knowledge recap answers

Learning aim A

1. Infancy, Early childhood, adolescence, Early adulthood, Middle adulthood, later adulthood

2. The hormonal changes in people as their bodies develop in adolescence in readiness for reproduction.

3. Sewing, sculpting, drawing, playing most musical instruments, using a crayon, pencil, brush, glue stick, manipulating clay, playdough, writing, cutting, threading, moving a cursor

4. Balancing, Crawling, Climbing, Jumping, Running, Twisting, Throwing, Walking, Catching, Leaping, Lifting

5. He is likely to start losing his hair. His strength will start to weaken and he will suffer more aches and pains. He will move more slowly and more carefully. He will be more fearful of things that didn't bother him at one time.

6. Abstract thinking is about general concepts and intuition. It is about looking at something and interpreting in many ways.
   Creative thinking is more focused and has an outcome in mind, for example to use lateral thinking come up with a new idea.

7. They have more memory capacity. There is still brain cell development whereas this stops in later life. They listen better and can concentrate better. They have not yet developed opinions that can hamper learning.

8. How a person sees themselves from knowledge of what they do and how other people see them. It often comes from comparisons with other people.

9. What a person feels about themselves, how much they like themselves and what they do. This can go up or down at any time.

10. So that they keep their minds and bodies active with fresh stimuli. If friendship groups disappear for whatever reason they have something to fall back on. They are not reliant on other people for anything unless it suits them. They may learn new skills and interest that take them away from friendship groups and which are more important in their development.

Learning aim B, Topic B.1

1. Character e.g. temperament. Diseases e.g. cystic fibrosis, more susceptible to breast cancer. Physical factors e.g. webbed feet, ear shape, hair colour.

2. If he stops smoking and takes up exercise he will save money. He should lose weight so he will feel better. He will be healthier. He is likely to need less medication now and in the future. He should live longer and have a better quality of life. He may not be able to do the exercise if he is still smoking. He may become disillusioned with it and give up the exercise completely AND the idea of dong exercise. The benefits of the exercise will not take place fully because the caused by smoking will still be there and are likely to be greater than the exercise benefits.

3. It depends on the severity of the virus and the strength of her immune system. Because a virus is not treated with antibiotics but rather left to the immune system, she should build up resistance to it and so her development will not be inhibited.

Topic B.2

1. They can learn good behaviour, skills, lifestyle habits such as diet and exercise, morals.

2. Bad habits that seem appealing such as challenging authority, being cheeky, bad manners, doing things to get noticed, overeating, smoking, wasting money, ego, must-have attitude, selfishness. These then become part of the person's persona and it is hard to change.

3. So that they can develop social skills such as communicating and sharing. They will pick up other skills such as seeing someone attempt a task e.g. climbing and learning how to do it from someone their own age. They will learn that they are not the only person in the world and that everyone has to have equal opportunity. These life skills need to be learned early so they become part of the child's persona.

Topic B.3

1. Part-time employment is where you work fewer hours than full time. It is regular and provides a constant known flow of income. Seasonal income only happens at times of labour shortage e.g. Christmas, so the income is temporary. The hours worked for seasonal employment may be similar to full time employment.

2. A job is something you do simply to gain money and will often not interest you nor will you necessarily do it for a long time. An occupation is employment where a trade is needed and where you will ply that trade in your working life albeit possibly with different companies e.g. a stonemason.

Topic B4

1. Wealth is something you inherit or accumulate over time and is often more than just money based e.g. land, paintings. Income is money you receive for doing a job.

2. Having a permanent contract for a job that guarantees your income and probably pension. It is not dependent on variable such as how may you sell but rather on the quality of the way you do your job.

3. Living in these sorts of conditions man there is always a greater likelihood of infection and disease. People will pick up viruses and bacterial infections more often and this will make their immune system work harder and it will sometimes let them down, or its effectiveness will be reduced. People are more likely to pick up serious disease such as typhoid which can have lasting affects on their lives. People living in poor conditions tend to live shorter lives and the quality of their life is often quite poor due to persistent ill-health.

Topic B.5

1. It's accepting a person for exactly who they are and to whether they fit a pre-conceived idea of what you think they should be. It's about removing prejudice and discrimination in our views about people and is about accepting them as they are because that is how they choose to be.

2. He may well have problems forming close relationships with other people as he may not have enjoyed much bonding as a child. He may be suspicious of people and wonder whether they are genuine and stable. On the other hand, he may have developed more sharing skills than allow him to interact better with a wider range of people. He may seek love more keenly if this has been missing in his early life.

Topic B.6

1. Getting married; getting divorced; parenthood,; retirement; going to school; getting a job

2. You can meet new friendship groups and develop new interests. This can put a new impetus into your life and cut down on complacency and boredom
It can be a new start and chance to get away from things that might have been a problem in your current house.
Sometimes it's a chance to upsize or downsize to a house more appropriate to your current needs which can have a boosting effect on morale.

3. You could miss out on the social interaction of work colleagues and possibly people you meet when travelling to work.
Retirement can sometimes make you feel you have become old and have nothing left to give to society; that you are nearing the end of your life.

Topic B.7

1. Death of a partner or friend; accident; ill health; promotion; unemployment

2. You get the chance to learn new skills maybe by having to take a new job or training. Sometimes it is the impetus to do something you had always wanted to do.
Quite often there is a financial compensation package which can act to help people set up a business or pay off their mortgage so they can afford to take a job that pays less but that they prefer.

3. By dropping out of education it sends out a poor message to some employers that you don't have a lot of staying power and that you leave when there is any pressure. Employers will often take a dim view of that approach. Even if it is not true many employers take a prejudiced view anyway. Evidence show that people who leave education early earn less than those who stay on. One reason is better qualifications will lead to better jobs but also more qualifications is seen as 'better' by some employers. They will only given interviews to people with certain qualifications so by leaving education early you may harm your chances of getting the chance to show what you can do.

Topic B.8

1. A community group is one that is bonded usually by how close people live to each other. They come together to support some sort of common interest e.g. neighbourhood watch or playgroups. A faith group is one united by that faith and wants to share those beliefs with each other and to others. They will often do many similar things to a community group e.g. counselling but often from a different starting point.

2. The social worker is independent and is likely to have fewer prejudices based on 'family'. The social worker is less likely to make judgements on what you are talking about than a family member would. Their advice will be impartial whereas a family member might be influenced by how others in the family would react. There is more likelihood that a social worker would keep a confidence as this is part of their job. As such you would probably tell them more, and be more honest, than you would a family member.

Unit 1 External assessment guidance: Answers

Section A

1. (a) Later adulthood

   (b) Early childhood

2. (a) To keep her fine motor skills working

   (b) To make sure her brain is working actively
   To maintain her independence
   To support her self-esteem
   To give her an interest where she may form a friendship/ interest group

3. (a) Parts of the body that develop with the intention of being involved in reproduction

   (b) Testes in men, ovaries in women

   (c) Men: facial hair, Adam's apple, deepening of voice, coarsening of skin
   Women: growth of breasts and nipples, widening of hips, more subcutaneous fat

   (d) She will start to have periods as puberty starts, becoming aware she could now have a baby.
   She will have mood swings as hormonal changes take place in her body which she cannot control but which she must manage.
   She will become more sexually aware of other people, how she is attracted to them and how they are attracted to her.

4. (a) May feel a lack of security
   May be a blow to her self-image
   May affect her self-esteem

   (b) Ariadne will have to learn new skills so she can tackle the new jobs and keep them, and make some money. These skills will help her move on in that area of employment if she so wishes. She could use them creatively maybe by setting up an agency to clean houses. Ariadne will have to develop her problem-solving ability if she is to move on to what she thinks is a more suitable or better job. She cannot sit back and do nothing as that will not change her life.

   (c) In the very short term the girls will not be affected (1) as they may well see more of Ariadne as she may be around the house more often when they are there (1).
   • After a while the girls may notice that there is less money available for luxuries (1) and they may come to resent this (1).
   • Some of the girls' friends may make nasty comments about their mum (1) and this could cause upset and anger (1).

   • The girls may feel let down (1) and become unpleasant towards their mum (1).
   • The girls may feel closer to their mum (1), depending on how well Ariadne communicates with them.
   • If Ariadne is out of the house a long time the girls may develop bad habits (1) and get into trouble (1).

Section B

1. (a) This was very appealing to Ian as the anorexia was always in the background (1) so the loss of weight made him feel much better about himself, as well as being much healthier. (1)

   (b) A disease is an alteration of the mental and/or physical structure of the human body or mind. (1). It is quite often a permanent problem. (1)
   • An illness is just feeling unwell and tends to be temporary (1) with no lasting effects (1). Illness can be the reaction to a disease (1) but a disease may be found if someone shows signs of illness. (1)

2. (a) Loss of income; unemployment; loss of trust; breakdown of relationships; stress.

   (b) The loss of income may mean they could not enjoy the lifestyle to which they had become accustomed (1). This would lead to resentment (1).
   • Unemployment may mean they would have to move house (1) so a lot of friendship groups might be lost (1).
   • The loss of trust may lead to family arguments (1) and things may never recover properly (1). The family would not encourage any other 'new' interest Ian had (1) and would constantly be checking up on him (1).
   • Family relationships could break down to the point where people stop talking (1) and then start to apportion blame for what happened (1)
   • Stress can build up, which can cause an illness in itself, (1) which will cause the situation to get worse (1).
   • When stressed, people say things they don't always mean (1) but by then it is too late. (1)

3. (a) She may start to lose muscle tone particularly if she cannot do as much exercise as before. (1)

She will face the menopause, which will affect her hormones and may cause some stress with hot flushes, drier skin and possibly loss of sleep **(1)**

(b) She may feel less useful to her family is she cannot do as much as she could when she was younger. This will lower her self-image and could lead to depression. **(1)**

However, as her family is now grown up she may feel a greater freedom so she can relax and enjoy her life more **(1)**.

Having the pacemaker fitted may make her think her life is nearing an end, which could depress her. **(1)**

Having a pacemaker fitted could make her reflect more on what is important and make her change her approach to life **(1)**

Relationships with family member may change e.g. if she becomes less interested in sex it may affect her marriage **(1)**

(c) She may be supported by her family if they understand her well and have her best interests at heart. However, they may not always give her the best advice as they might be frightened of upsetting her if she is fragile. So although they may look and sound concerned they might not be able to give the best support.

On the other hand, formal support, for example from a GP, might give her more practical and useful advice that is not biased by any emotions. However, because of that very fact the professional care may not be able to take into account outside factors such as her relationship with her spouse.

Both forms of support have benefits and drawbacks. Both rely on her being open, honest and giving them the full picture. She may not feel able to speak freely to either party so that will inhibit the way they can support her. For example, she may not want to tell the GP about parts of her private life, whilst she may not tell her family the whole story of her physical state if she doesn't want to worry them.

4. (a) Retirement gives them the chance to do what they want and when they want to. This will be a benefit as they can take advantage of cheap flights, etc. They can enjoy history visits at their own pace when it is quieter, such as in school terms. This will be very relaxing as they can spend whatever time is needed.

On the other hand, they will have a lower income so they may have to watch the finances a bit. That may stop them from doing certain things. Depending on how they have lived so far this may be OK if they are naturally frugal.

Although they are married they may not before have to spend all day, every day together, had and that might prove a strain. One or both may have to make changes, e.g. get a part-time job, if their relationship starts to suffer.

Having more time to spend doing what they want should make them happier as employment pressures have gone, as well as the pressures of raising a family. They may be able to take up new hobbies, which will be even more fulfilling.

Overall, they will need to make some changes. Some might be easier than others but if they can get the balance right and make sure they remain active in some way they should enjoy their retirement without ending up in poverty.

Unit 2 Knowledge recap answers

Learning aim A

1. Ensuring that personal information is kept safely and is accessible only to those who are authorised to have access to it.
2. Any three from: safe storage of records; non-disclosure to unauthorised persons; not sharing information without permission; right to anonymity.
3. Because Lily has a right to confidentiality. Nobody else has a 'right' to that information, for example, a parent. If the nurse breaches this confidence she will be acting illegally and other people may not trust her.
4. A decision should not be influenced by any factors other than the facts as presented. For

example, a person's age, gender or ethnicity should not affect the decision.

5. Not making any assumptions in advance about the client or the situation. Not allowing personal opinion to influence what is the best for the client.

6. So that you do not make or show any assumptions about her marital status. This is a generic title used to address women.

7. Because he is there to look after them, not the other way round. He has to focus upon respecting their needs. Telling them his problems is inappropriate. It could make them feel worse if they themselves are not well. He needs to be person-centred.

8. Ensuring that anything you do does not intentionally harm anyone else and ensuring that you do not act in a negligent way by ignoring risks.

9. Protecting people from being maltreated and ensuring they can develop properly and safely. Ensuring they can live in a safe and secure environment, for example elderly people being looked after in a registered and inspected care home or children being safe in school as all staff have had a CRB check.

10. Physical safety is ensuring that risks of accidents within the environment are minimised, for example by having fire exits, sprinklers, etc. Emotional safety is ensuring things such as bullying are eliminated; that people in fragile mental situations are treated properly; that people's feelings are taken into account during any treatment.

Learning aim B

1. So that employees feel more valued, more satisfied with their jobs and so they will put in an extra effort as they know they are valued.

2. Sue has a right to privacy in a situation that causes her embarrassment and stress. This is a reasonable request and the supervisor should arrange for someone else to do it. Sue has not objected to being bathed by someone, just to the male carer. It is not a personal issue with the carers. By taking this into account the supervisor can plan well and respect everyone's feelings, particularly Sue who will feel more valued.

3. Makaton is a system that uses signs and symbols to help people to communicate. It supports spoken language, and the signs and symbols are used with speech, in spoken word order. The idea is that people stop using Makaton when speech develops as the preferred method of communication.

4. To ensure all potential problems and issues have been identified and that as many ways of avoiding them can be put in place as possible. Recognising possible issues is the key. Also, by carrying out a risk assessment the care home is covered legally to some extent should a problem arise. There is evidence of what had been identified and what practices had been put in place. It benefits both the resident and the business itself, ensuring that the resident gets the best possible and most appropriate care.

Index